DK SMITHSONIAN ✺

KIDS' FIELD GUIDES

Birds

of North America WEST

Jo S. Kittinger

SMITHSONIAN

LONDON, NEW YORK, SYDNEY, DELHI, PARIS,
MUNICH, and JOHANNESBURG

Editor-in-Chief Russell Greenberg, Ph.D.
Director of the Migratory Bird Center at the National Zoological Park

Publisher Andrew Berkhut
Project Editor Andrea Curley
Art Director Tina Vaughan
Jacket Designer Karen Shooter

Produced by Southern Lights Custom Publishing
Editorial Director Shelley DeLuca
Production Director Lee Howard
Art Director Miles Parsons
President Ellen Sullivan

Editorial Consultants
Joseph DiCostanzo
Alice S. Christenson, Frank Farrell III, Shirley J. Farrell
Dana Hamilton, Stan Hamilton, Greg Harber

First American Edition, 2001
00 01 02 03 04 05   10 9 8 7 6 5 4 3 2 1
Published in the United States by
DK Publishing, Inc.
95 Madison Avenue, New York, New York 10016
Copyright © 2001 DK Publishing, Inc. and Smithsonian Institution

Library of Congress Cataloging-in-Publication Data
Kittinger, Jo S.
Birds of North America. West / by Jo S. Kittinger.--1st American ed.
p. cm. -- (Smithsonian kid's field guides)
ISBN 0-7894-7901-X (pp) ISBN 0-7894-7900-1 (lib. bdg.)
1. Birds--West (U.S.)--Identification--Juvenile literature. 2. Birds--Canada,
Eastern--Identification--Juvenile literature. [1. Birds--Identification.] I. Title. II. Series.

QL683.W4 K58 2001
598'.0978--dc21   2001028430

Printed and bound in Italy by Graphicom, srl.
Color reproduction by Colourscan, Singapore.

see our complete catalog at
www.dk.com

Contents

How to Use This Book

Using this book, you will learn to identify 140 birds that you might find near you in western North America. Each page tells what the bird looks like, where it lives, how it sounds, and what it eats.

THE PICTURES

The photos in this book show you the colors of a bird's feathers in spring and summer, called breeding plumage. This is when birds reproduce, or breed. When males and females look very different at this time, you will see a photo of each. When birds are finished breeding, they grow their winter plumage. Like the goldfinch at right, some can look different in winter. Also, a young bird, called a juvenile, can look different from its parents. Some birds, such as gulls, take up to four years to look like an adult. Drawings like these show these differences.

Winter male

Winter female

Juvenile

THE MAP

Each page has a map like this. The colors tell you what time of year that bird might be in your area. But remember that although some birds stay in one place all year, others move around. This is called migration. If you live somewhere in between two colors, you might see that bird during migration in the spring and fall.

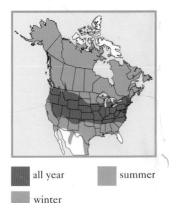

all year   summer

winter

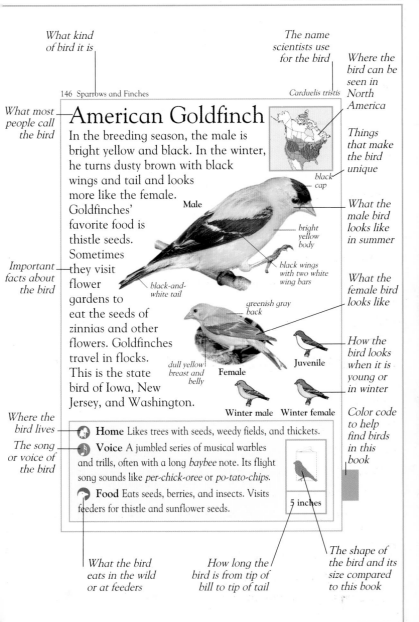

What kind of bird it is

The name scientists use for the bird

Where the bird can be seen in North America

146 Sparrows and Finches

Carduelis tristis

What most people call the bird

American Goldfinch

In the breeding season, the male is bright yellow and black. In the winter, he turns dusty brown with black wings and tail and looks more like the female. Goldfinches' favorite food is thistle seeds. Sometimes they visit flower gardens to eat the seeds of zinnias and other flowers. Goldfinches travel in flocks. This is the state bird of Iowa, New Jersey, and Washington.

Things that make the bird unique

black cap

Male

What the male bird looks like in summer

bright yellow body

black wings with two white wing bars

black-and-white tail

greenish gray back

What the female bird looks like

Important facts about the bird

dull yellow breast and belly

Female

Juvenile

How the bird looks when it is young or in winter

Winter male   Winter female

Color code to help find birds in this book

Where the bird lives

🏠 **Home** Likes trees with seeds, weedy fields, and thickets.

The song or voice of the bird

🎵 **Voice** A jumbled series of musical warbles and trills, often with a long *baybee* note. Its flight song sounds like *per-chick-oree* or *po-tato-chips*.

🌿 **Food** Eats seeds, berries, and insects. Visits feeders for thistle and sunflower seeds.

5 inches

What the bird eats in the wild or at feeders

How long the bird is from tip of bill to tip of tail

The shape of the bird and its size compared to this book

About Birds

There are more than 9,000 species of birds in the world. They all have several things in common. All birds are warm-blooded. All birds are covered with feathers. All birds have two legs, usually covered with scaly skin. All birds have two wings, but not all birds can fly. All birds have a bill, but no teeth. All birds lay eggs.

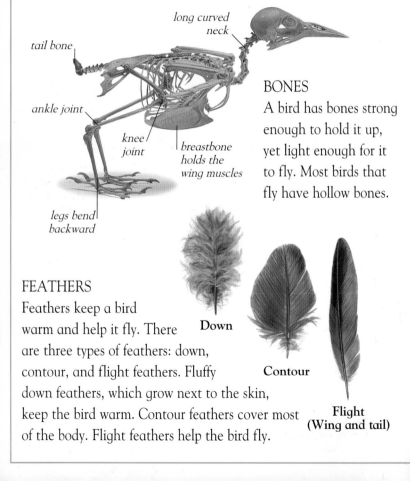

long curved neck

tail bone

ankle joint

knee joint

breastbone holds the wing muscles

legs bend backward

BONES
A bird has bones strong enough to hold it up, yet light enough for it to fly. Most birds that fly have hollow bones.

Down

Contour

Flight (Wing and tail)

FEATHERS
Feathers keep a bird warm and help it fly. There are three types of feathers: down, contour, and flight feathers. Fluffy down feathers, which grow next to the skin, keep the bird warm. Contour feathers cover most of the body. Flight feathers help the bird fly.

BILLS

Birds use their bills to clean themselves, to build a nest, and to eat. The shape of the bill determines what the bird can eat.

Osprey
Birds of prey use their strong hooked bills to eat meat or fish.

American Robin
Thrushes and other songbirds use their pointed bills to pick up berries and insects.

Northern Shoveler

Ducks, which strain food out of the water, have flat bills.

LEGS AND FEET

Bird legs are thin, but strong. Most bird have four toes, with three toes pointing forward and one turned to the back. A claw is on each toe. A bird's feet are made for its lifestyle, whether that is perching, hunting, or swimming.

The American Robin has three toes forward and one toe back for perching on branches.

The Osprey has claws, called talons, that are good for holding its prey.

The Northern Shoveler has webs between three toes to help the duck paddle through water.

Identifying Birds

Most birds do not sit still for long. To identify birds it is important to notice details quickly. Practice asking yourself these questions, because the answers are what you need to name the birds you see.

WHAT SHAPE AND SIZE IS THE BIRD?
The first things you should look at are a bird's shape and size. This will help you place the bird in a family group and locate it in this book, using the symbols in the bottom right corner of the page.

WHAT COLORS ARE THE FEATHERS?
Is the bird blue or brown? This can point you in the right direction, but it is also important to notice whether the feathers are spotted, streaked, or plain.

spotted   streaked   plain and unmarked

WHAT DOES THE HEAD LOOK LIKE?
Look at the shape and the markings.

The point on top of the head of a Stellar's Jay is called a crest.

The Loggerhead Shrike looks like it is wearing a mask on its face.

WHAT DOES THE BILL LOOK LIKE?

Look at the shape and the color.

The American Coot is a gray ducklike bird with a white bill.

The Common Snipe's bill is twice as long as its head.

WHAT DO THE LEGS LOOK LIKE?

Look at the color.

The Great Egret holds its black legs behind its body when it flies.

The Herring Gull has pink legs.

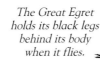

WHAT DO THE WINGS LOOK LIKE?

Look at the shape, size, and markings.

A Prairie Falcon has long, pointed wings.

The large white patches on the Northern Mockingbird's wings make the bird easy to identify in flight.

WHAT DOES THE TAIL LOOK LIKE?

Look at the shape, size, and markings.

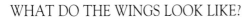

The Band-tailed Pigeon has a square tail with a band on it.

The Black-billed Magpie has a very long tail with green highlights.

HABITS

While you look at a bird you should also notice what it is doing. Like people who have habits such as tugging their hair or tapping their fingers, birds have habits that can be great clues to their identity. Does the bird hover in the air? Does it wag its tail? Does it climb up, or down, a tree? All of these habits, or behaviors, can help you learn a bird's identity.

Wrens often hold their tails up.

Nuthatches climb headfirst down trees.

Meadowlarks can be heard singing their loud song in fields.

♪ VOICE

Experienced birdwatchers can identify birds by their song or call. Not all birds sing, but most of them do make noise. Many birds have a call, which is different from the song. A call is simple and might mean the bird is frightened. Birds may use calls to communicate. In this book you can read about a bird's song where you see the symbol above.

FOOD

Birds live in places where they can find the food they need to survive. Some birds pick fruits and berries from trees. Others look in or near the water for food. Find out what a bird eats where you see the symbol above.

Sanderlings are often seen on saltwater beaches, looking for food at the edge of the water.

🌲 HOME

Most birds have a particular place where they like to live, called a habitat. The beach is a habitat of sand, saltwater, and the plants and animals that live there. Identifying birds is easier if you learn which birds to expect in different habitats. After you look at the range map on each page to see where a bird lives, read about its habitat where you see the symbol above. But remember that during migration birds can appear in unlikely places.

Flocks of American Crows gather in large, open places such as prairies or fields.

Watching Birds

Watching birds, "birding," is something you can do anywhere. The best times are early in the morning or late in the afternoon, when birds are most active. Remember to be as still and quiet as you can, because

A pair of binoculars will help you see birds up close.

quick moves and noise will scare birds away. It is also helpful if you wear dull colors so you will blend in with nature. Be sure to take along this book, binoculars, and a notebook and pencil.

PATTERNS IN THE AIR

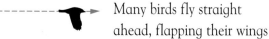

Many birds fly straight ahead, flapping their wings the whole time. This is true of ducks, doves, crows, and many songbirds. The heavier a bird is, the faster it needs to fly to stay in the air.

Some birds flap their wings several times, then glide.

This helps save energy. Birds that flap and glide are hawks, owls, vultures, and pelicans.

Many smaller birds, such as woodpeckers and chickadees, hold their wings close to their bodies as they pause and glide between flaps. This makes them fly up and down like a roller coaster.

KEEP YOUR DISTANCE
Watching birds is fun, but you do not want to get too close. If you find a bird's nest, be sure to watch it from a distance. Do not touch it. Birders are always careful not to disturb wildlife of any kind.

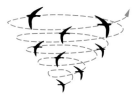

Another way some birds save energy is by soaring. Large hawks, eagles, vultures, and gulls ride upward on heated air (which rises) or drafts.

Certain types of birds can flap their wings rapidly while staying in the same place in the air. Hummingbirds do this

while gathering flower nectar. Some birds of prey, such as the American Kestrel, hover in the air while looking for food.

Some birds fly in straight lines or V-shaped patterns to help save energy. By riding on the air flowing from the bird in front of it, the bird behind does not have to flap its wings as hard.

Bringing Birds Home

Attracting birds to your backyard will let you enjoy their habits, colors, and songs. By putting out food, water, and shelter you can help provide a good habitat for these beautiful creatures.

FOOD

Invite birds to your yard with food. The foods you can put out to attract them are listed in the bird descriptions. Some birds like to eat on the ground. Others will come to feeders that are filled with seeds, suet, or nectar. Many types of birdfeeders are available at stores.

American Goldfinches eat at feeders that are filled with thistle or sunflower seeds.

Woodpeckers such as this Downy Woodpecker will come to eat from your suet feeder.

Many birds, such as these Mourning Doves, prefer to eat their food on the ground. No feeder is required – just throw down some black oil sunflower seeds and watch the birds eat.

WATER

Do not forget water! Birds need a supply of water for drinking and bathing. Regular baths help a bird keep itself clean and maintain its feathers.

Bluebirds depend on nest boxes like this one for a place to raise their young. Inside the nest box, the baby birds wait for a meal.

SHELTER

Before you can give birds a home, you need to find out what kinds of birds in your area might use it. Different families of birds make different sizes and shapes of nests. They use all kinds of nest-building materials. You can help birds build a cozy nest by putting nesting materials such as string or dryer lint outside where birds can find it. Look in books or on the Internet to find instructions for all types of nest boxes.

Great Blue Heron

This bird is the largest heron in North America. Like all herons, it flies with its neck held in an S-shape. A heron usually stands very still in the water before stabbing prey with its daggerlike bill.

black crown

yellowish bill

dark streaks on whitish neck

bluish gray body

Juvenile

In flight the heron's long legs reach far past its tail.

long yellow-green legs

🌲 **Home** Lives near shallow water of rivers, lakes, swamps, and ponds. Also lives along the coast. Sometimes it may be seen walking in grassy fields near water. Many pairs of birds make their nests close together in the same tree.

🎵 **Voice** Usually silent except around other herons, when it makes squawks and low croaks.

🐟 **Food** Eats fish, frogs, salamanders, snakes, grasshoppers, mice, dragonflies, and squirrels.

46–52 inches

Great Egret

In January both the male and female Great Egret grow long, white plumes on their backs to attract a mate. The birds shed their beautiful plumes by summer and do not have any for the rest of the year.

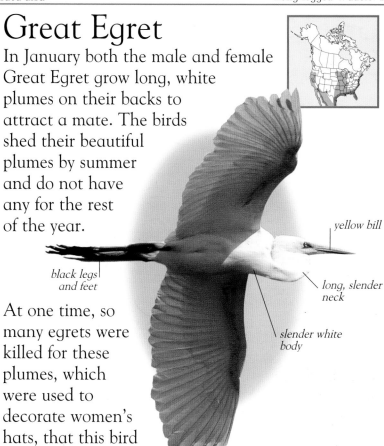

yellow bill

black legs and feet

long, slender neck

slender white body

At one time, so many egrets were killed for these plumes, which were used to decorate women's hats, that this bird almost became extinct.

Home Lives near freshwater ponds and marshes. Also lives near saltwater marshes as well as along the coast.

Voice Croaks loudly or says *cuk, cuk.*

Food Eats fish, frogs, snakes, crayfish, and large insects.

37–41 inches

Green Heron

This bird is a natural fisherman. The Green Heron will actually place some bait – a feather or twig – in the water to lure fish and other small prey, such as frogs. The Green Heron eats alone or in pairs. It can stand still for minutes at a time while looking for food. The bird might raise the crest of dark green feathers on its head when it is nervous or excited.

dark green head

crest that can be raised

blue-green back

thin brownish yellow bill

chestnut neck

yellow or orange legs

Juvenile

🌲 **Home** Lives near wetlands, including swamps, marshes, ponds, and wooded streams.

🎵 **Voice** Sounds like *kyowk* or *skeow* or a quieter *kuck, kuck*.

🐦 **Food** Eats mostly small fish but also eats insects and frogs.

18–22 inches

Black-crowned Night-Heron

This active night hunter sometimes flies to the nests of other birds to eat their young. You might see a large colony roosting together in trees during the day. Conservation groups are trying to protect the night-heron, but its wetland habitats are shrinking. A similar bird, the Yellow-crowned Night-Heron, lives in the Southeast. It has a yellowish stripe on its crown, a black face, and a gray back.

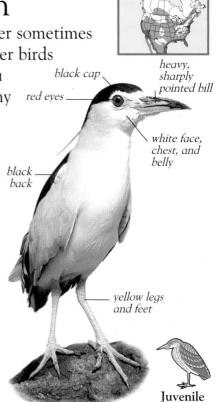

black cap

red eyes

heavy, sharply pointed bill

white face, chest, and belly

black back

yellow legs and feet

Juvenile

🌲 **Home** Lives in wetlands, marshes, swamps, streams near woods, and near the coast.

🎵 **Voice** Sounds like a loud *quock* or *quaik*.

🐟 **Food** Prefers small fish but also eats snakes, frogs, mice, and sometimes young birds. This bird also walks through tall grass, looking for mice.

25–28 inches

White-faced Ibis

Pesticides once made it difficult for the White-faced Ibis to reproduce. These poisons thinned the bird's eggshells, and many eggs did not hatch. Now that certain pesticides are illegal, more eggs are hatching. A flock of ibises flies in a straight line, looking like a long line of question marks.

bare red skin between bill and red eye

dark chestnut-colored back

bill curves downward

bronze-and-green belly

reddish legs

🌲 **Home** Lives near marshes and along the coast. Nests and roosts in trees, in different places every year.

🎵 **Voice** When feeding, it makes an oinking sound. At other times, its call sounds like a low *graa, graa, graa.*

🌑 **Food** Eats insects, crayfish, frogs, and fish.

20–26 inches

Sandhill Crane

This is the only crane that can be found in many places across North America. It flies with its neck held straight out in front. In spring these birds pair off and do an amazing dance. They jump in the air, spread their wings, and call loudly. Another member of the crane family is the larger Whooping Crane, which is white with black wing tips and a black mustache. The Whooping Crane is endangered.

red crown

white cheeks, chin, and upper throat

long neck

Juvenile

gray body and wings

long blackish legs and feet

🌲 **Home** Lives near shallow ponds, marshes, lakes with forests nearby, and damp meadows.

🎵 **Voice** Its loud, trumpetlike *garoo-oo-a-a-a-a* can be heard from more than a mile away.

🐟 **Food** Eats small birds, snakes, lizards, frogs, mice, and crayfish. Also eats water plants, berries, seeds, and grains.

34–48 inches

Common Loon

A loon can see underwater. This is helpful, because a loon can dive as deep as 200 feet below the surface and can stay underwater for as long as three minutes. Since loons spend so much time on lakes, a healthy loon can be a sign of clean water. This is the state bird of Minnesota and the official bird of Ontario.

shiny black head with green gloss

checkered black-and-white back

striped white neck

white breast and belly

In winter another member of the loon family, the Red-throated Loon, looks like a small Common Loon with a plain gray back.

Winter adult

🌲 **Home** Lives in lakes and rivers near forests in summer. In winter, moves to the ocean or coast.

🎵 **Voice** Known for the spooky laughing sounds it makes. Also yodels, sounding like *ha-oo-oo*.

🌑 **Food** Eats fish, shrimp, snails, and frogs.

28–36 inches

Eared Grebe

The "ears" are two golden tufts of feathers behind the eyes. This bird is social and gathers in groups of up to several hundred pairs. Male and female do a "penguin dance" side-by-side on the water when they begin to pick a mate. Another member of this family, the Horned Grebe, looks similar.

head shaped like a triangle

thin bill

golden "ears"

black neck

During winter the neck turns dusky gray, and the feathers on the chest and belly turn white.

Winter plumage

🌲 **Home** Lives mostly in lakes and ponds in western and southwestern United States. Winters along coast.

🎵 **Voice** Makes a soft *poo-ee-chk* and a shriek.

🐦 **Food** Dives and swims underwater to find food. Eats water bugs in freshwater and shrimplike crustaceans in saltwater.

12–13 inches

American White Pelican

This is the largest water bird in North America, and one of two kinds of pelicans. A pelican flies with its head resting on its shoulders.

pale-yellow crest

black wing tips

large orange bill

Flocks of white pelicans may "herd" fish into shallow water in order to scoop the fish into the big pouches in their bills.

Winter plumage

🌲 **Home** In summer, lives on western lakes. In winter this bird can be found in the southwestern and Gulf Coast states.

🎵 **Voice** Mostly silent except during nesting, when it makes guttural croaks.

🌑 **Food** Eats mostly fish.

60–63 inches

Double-crested Cormorant

A cormorant may look like a duck, but it is more closely related to a pelican. Like the pelican, a cormorant has webs on its feet that reach to its toes. Unlike pelicans and ducks, a cormorant's wings are not waterproof. After it finishes fishing, a cormorant has to go ashore, where it perches with its wings open so they can dry. Then the bird can fly well again.

tufts in breeding season

bright yellow-orange throat pouch

brown back with black feathers

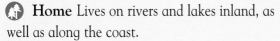

🏕 **Home** Lives on rivers and lakes inland, as well as along the coast.

🎵 **Voice** Makes a deep, guttural grunt.

🌑 **Food** Dives and swims underwater to catch and eat fish and shrimp.

32 inches

Snow Goose

This bird comes in two different color morphs. There is a completely white one with black tips on its wings and a dark one with a bluish gray upper body and brownish gray lower body. The dark morph is called the "Blue Goose." The Snow Goose often feeds in fields far away from water.

black wing tips

Dark morph adult

pink bill

black patch on edges of bill looks like a grin

white body

White morph juvenile

Dark morph juvenile

🏠 **Home** In summer, lives in the northern tundra of Canada. Flies south to the eastern and western coasts of the US in winter. Nests in large colonies. Sometimes there are as many as 1,200 nests in one square mile.

🎵 **Voice** Makes either shrill or soft honks. In flight it makes a barking sound.

🌓 **Food** Eats tender plants and grains in winter. Digs up and eats roots of water plants in summer.

25–31 inches

Canada Goose

If you hear honking and look up to see several geese flying in a V shape, they are probably Canada Geese. They come in different sizes, and some people call the bigger geese "honkers." There are more of this species than any other kind of goose, and they are probably increasing in number.

brownish gray back

white "strap" on chin

paler brown sides

light-colored belly

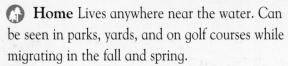

🏠 **Home** Lives anywhere near the water. Can be seen in parks, yards, and on golf courses while migrating in the fall and spring.

🎵 **Voice** Deep musical *honk-a-lonk* or cackling.

🍂 **Food** Eats fresh grasses and other plants.

25–45 inches

Tundra Swan

The Tundra Swan builds its nest
and raises its young on the tundra,
the cold arctic plains in Alaska and
Canada. It flies south in flocks to
spend the winter near the coast,
where the weather is warmer.
This swan can be found on
both sides of the continent but
is more common in the East.
Also called the "Whistling
Swan," it is the smallest
swan in North
America.

black bill
curves
down at tip

yellow or orange
spot between
eye and bill

white body

Juvenile

Home Lives near bays or freshwater lakes.

Voice Sounds like yodeling or soft, musical
laughter, *wow-HOW-ow*.

Food Dips its long neck and head underwater
to eat water plants and dig up their roots. Also
eats grass found on dry land.

47–58
inches

Wood Duck

The colorful Wood Duck is named for the wooded habitat where it lives. It is called a "perching duck" because it perches in trees. Sharp claws help the Wood Duck hold onto branches. Like most other ducks, the female Wood Duck is less colorful than her mate.

gray head

white circle around the eyes

brownish chest

Female

Juvenile

big pointed crest

red, white, black, and yellow bill

blue-green back

Male

long tail

dark-red chest with white spots

yellowish sides

🏃 **Home** Lives near wooded rivers, ponds, and swamps. Visits marshes in summer and fall. Nests in tree cavities. Also uses nest boxes people make for them.

🎵 **Voice** Male whistles a soft *jeee?* or *ter-weeee?* Female loudly says *wooo-eek!*

🦅 **Food** Eats water plants, snails, tadpoles, salamanders, acorns, seeds, and grains.

17–20 inches

Anas platyrhynchos

Mallard

This familiar duck can be found near shallow freshwater almost anywhere in North America. The shiny green head, purplish breast, and white collar of the male are in sharp contrast to the dull brown spotted feathers of the female.

shiny green head

Male

purplish breast

white sides and belly

orange-and-brown speckled bill

blue-purple patch with white edges

Female

🏠 **Home** Lives near ponds, marshes, and lakes. Tame Mallards can be found on any body of water, sometimes even in city parks, pastures, or alfalfa fields.

🎵 **Voice** Female has a loud *quack-quack-quack* that sounds softer the longer she speaks. Male makes a double *kwek-kwek-kwek*.

🌙 **Food** Dabbles, or turns upside down, in shallow water to find plants and insects. Also looks for food on the shore or in a nearby field.

23 inches

Cinnamon Teal

Teals are small ducks that dabble for food, swishing their bills in the water with the tail tipped up. This teal is common in western marshes. Like all ducks, the female is plain and brown so she can hide in her nest.

brown body

Female

cinnamon head and neck

orange eye

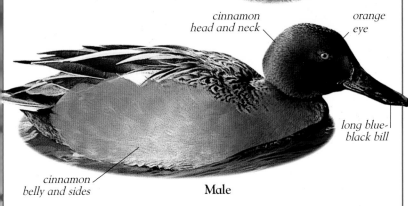

long blue-black bill

cinnamon belly and sides

Male

🏠 **Home** Lives near marshes, creeks, ponds, and streams lined with cattails and reeds.

🎵 **Voice** Makes a soft quacking noise. Also clucks and chatters in low notes.

🌑 **Food** Skims the water with its bill to gather and eat seeds of underwater plants, snails, and crustaceans. Also eats wild rice and corn.

14–17 inches

Anas clypeata

Northern Shoveler

The shoveler has a bill that is longer and wider than any other duck's bill. It is shaped like a shovel with ridges on the side. The bird pushes it through the water to find food.

Male

white tail feathers

black head with green shine

white spot on flank

rusty red sides and belly

Three or four shovelers may swim in a circle so they can eat the food stirred up by the feet in front of them.

gray bill with orange speckles

brown speckled back

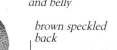

Female

🏠 **Home** Needs water to find food. Spends winter in freshwater marshes. Nests in spring in small ponds or prairie potholes.

🎵 **Voice** Usually quiet but sometimes makes low quacking sounds.

🌑 **Food** Eats water plants and animals.

17–20 inches

Lesser Scaup

This expert diver is common in North America. In winter, scaups float on the water in a large flock called a "raft." Like other diving ducks, a scaup needs a running start on the water before it can take off. A similar duck, the Greater Scaup, might be seen with Lesser Scaups in winter but it is less common.

white on face

brown body

Female

pointed black head

gray back

Male

bluish gray bill has black tip

black chest

🏠 **Home** Lives near ponds and marshes, as well as in bays and inlets. In the winter, visits lakes and rivers.

🎵 **Voice** The male whistles a low *whew* when looking for a mate. The female purrs *kwuh-h-h-h*.

🍃 **Food** Eats weeds, grass, snails, shrimplike crustaceans, and water insects.

15–18 inches

Bucephala albeola

Bufflehead

The Bufflehead is the smallest diving duck. It can take off directly from the water, which is unusual because most diving ducks need to get a running start on the water first. Buffleheads do not form large flocks in winter like some diving ducks. When looking for a mate, the male puts on a show, bobbing his head up and down.

white chest and belly

gray-brown body

Female

white on back of head

green or purple face

black back

Male

white chest and belly

🌲 **Home** Likes to spend winters on the coast. In summer, lives near ponds, lakes, and rivers.

🎵 **Voice** Has a squeaky whistle and sometimes makes a low squealing or growling. Females quack.

🦆 **Food** Dives for water insects, snails, small fish, underwater plant seeds, and shrimp.

13–16 inches

Common Merganser

Of all the ducks that dive into the water to catch and eat fish, the merganser is the largest. Its narrow bill has "teeth" on the sides that help this bird hold onto slippery fish. Because of these teeth some people call the Common Merganser by the nickname "Sawbill."

tufted chestnut head

gray body

white chin

Female

Male

glossy green head

black back

thin red bill

long body

white belly and chest

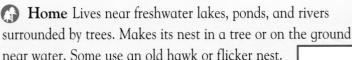

🐦 **Home** Lives near freshwater lakes, ponds, and rivers surrounded by trees. Makes its nest in a tree or on the ground near water. Some use an old hawk or flicker nest.

🎵 **Voice** Male croaks harshly. Female loudly says *karr karr.*

🍂 **Food** Eats mostly fish, especially minnows, plus eels, frogs, salamanders, and water insects.

22–27 inches

Ruddy Duck

This little diving duck can sink slowly underwater and disappear without leaving any ripples in the water. It uses its long, stiff tail to steer in the water like a boat uses a rudder. The Ruddy Duck is better suited for swimming than walking. Its legs are so far back on its body that it is almost helpless on land.

brown-gray back

blackish gray bill **Female**

white cheeks

blue bill

whitish belly

blackish head

Male

long, stiff tail

rust-colored body

Winter male

🏠 **Home** Lives near marshes surrounded by cattails and reeds. Also along the coast during winter.

🎵 **Voice** Mostly silent, but a male trying to find a mate says *chuck-chuck-chuck-chuck-churr*.

🐟 **Food** Dives into water to find shellfish and water plants. Also eats grass found in ponds.

14–16 inches

American Coot

Even though it looks like a duck, this is a member of the rail family. Coots are usually seen in large flocks swimming on large bodies of water. The American Coot pumps its head back and forth while it is swimming.

reddish brown patch on forehead

gray-black head and neck

short white bill

dark-gray body

This bird is a bit of a bully and sometimes steals from other birds that dive into the water for food.

Juvenile

> 🏠 **Home** Lives near marshes, lakes, ponds, rivers, and coasts.
>
> 🎵 **Voice** Cackles, whistles, and grunts while splashing in water. Also says *coo-coo-coo-coo.*
>
> 🐦 **Food** Dives 10–25 feet below water for plants, small fish, tadpoles, snails, and worms.

15 inches

Sooty Shearwater

A shearwater glides so close to the water that the wings look as if they might cut the surface like a pair of shears, or scissors. This is how the shearwater got its name. During migration, thousands of these birds rest together, making a giant black mass on the water. From shore you also might see them flying in long, circling lines. A tube on the top of the bill helps get rid of extra salt in the bird's body.

long, slender dark wings

silvery gray underwing

long, hooked dark bill

dark grayish-brown body

🌲 **Home** Stays mostly on the ocean. Colonies nest in burrows on islands in the Southern Hemisphere.

🎵 **Voice** Mostly silent. Squeals when fighting over food. Makes crooning *koo-wah-koo-wah* sounds near nests.

🐟 **Food** Dives to catch small fish, squid, and other small sea animals.

18–20 inches

Semipalmated Plover

You are most likely to see this small shorebird when it migrates. In spring and fall, flocks move between their summer breeding grounds in the Far North and their winter home on southern beaches.

faint eye ring

brown back

orange bill with black tip

broad black collar

white chest and belly

orange or yellow legs

some webbing between toes

A Semipalmated Plover searches for its food by running, then stopping suddenly. The American Robin behaves similarly when it is eating.

Home Lives near beaches, lakes, and rivers.

Voice Gives a clear, whistled *chee-wee, chur-wee, chu-weet,* or *tyoo-eep.*

Food Along the sea coast it eats small shellfish and the eggs of marine animals. Inland it eats a lot of grasshoppers.

7.25 inches

Charadrius vociferus

Killdeer

The Killdeer is named for its loud cry, which can sound like *kill-deear*. It is the only plover in its range that has two bands across its chest. The Killdeer is one of many shorebirds that perform the "crippled bird act" if their nests or young are threatened.

orange eye ring

gray-brown head and back

thin black bill

bright reddish orange rump

white belly and chest

two black bands across chest

creamy pink legs and feet

The bird calls rapidly, drags its wings, spreads its tail, and even limps to one side to distract the intruder. When the intruder has left the area, the bird is "healed" and flies away.

Home Lives along river banks and near golf courses, fields, and neighborhood lawns.

Voice Loud cry sounds like *kill-deear* or *kill-deeah-dee-dee*. Also makes a long, trilled *trrrrrrrr* during its "crippled bird act."

Food Runs, stops, and stands still, then stabs at the ground with its bill to catch insects.

9–10.5 inches

Black Oystercatcher

The oystercatcher does eat oysters, but it eats other types of shellfish, too. This large bird has a strong, flattened red-orange bill with a sharp tip. The tip is shaped like a chisel, which the bird uses to pry open the shells of its food.

yellow eyes

black or dark-brown body

long, straight, flat bright red-orange bill

The bill is more than twice as long as the bird's head. While other shorebirds feed in flocks with other species, this bird feeds alone or in small groups of its own.

pink legs and feet

Home Lives along the Pacific Coast from Baja California to the Aleutian Islands in Alaska.

Voice Makes a loud *keee, kee-ah* and a rapid series of *tees, whee-whee-tee-tee-tee*.

Food Eats shellfish and marine worms.

17.5 inches

American Avocet

The avocet sweeps its long bill back and forth in shallow water to stir up its food. The bird keeps its bill partly open to filter the food from the water. Avocets feed in flocks. You might see these birds walking shoulder to shoulder with their bills in the water, all moving their heads back and forth at the same time.

cinnamon-colored head and neck

black-and-white back and wings

long, thin, up-curved bill

white chest and belly

In deeper water they feed like ducks by tipping over into the water bill-first.

long blue-gray legs

Winter adult

🌲 **Home** In summer lives near lakes and rivers, and sometimes grasslands. In winter lives at the seashore, in marshes, ponds, and lakes.

🎵 **Voice** Loudly calls *wheet* or *pleeet*.

🐟 **Food** Eats water insects as well as shrimp and other crustaceans.

18–20 inches

Greater Yellowlegs

When it is frightened, the Greater Yellowlegs whistles a loud alarm call. Other shorebirds respond to this alarm as a warning. This gray sandpiper can be identified by its large size, white tail, and long bright-yellow legs.

long grayish bill

dark gray-brown back with white speckles

long, slender neck

white breast and belly with brown speckles and bars

A similar bird, the Lesser Yellowlegs, is smaller and thinner and has a straighter and shorter bill.

long bright-yellow legs

🏠 **Home** Lives in open marshes and near ponds, streams, or flooded fields and golf courses.

🎵 **Voice** Makes a loud, repeated *teu-teu-teu* that goes down in pitch. Also sings *too-whee* to let other birds know about its territory.

🦞 **Food** Eats small fish, insects, crabs, and snails.

14 inches

Willet

The best way to identify this member of the sandpiper family is by the black-and-white pattern on its wings. You might see this bird standing on one leg, sleeping with its head tucked into the feathers on its back. Near its nesting area the Willet sometimes perches high on rocks, posts, or other tall objects so it can look for intruders.

white ring around eyes goes to bill

bold black-and-white pattern on wings

blue-gray legs and feet

Winter adult

🏠 **Home** Lives on sandy seashore or in freshwater marshes.

🎵 **Voice** Calls *pill-will-will; pill-o-will-o-willet;* or *pill-will-willet.* When disturbed by an intruder, it calls *kip* or *wiek.* Calls out *wee-wee-weet* in flight.

🌓 **Food** In the water it eats insects, marine worms, crabs, mollusks, and small fish. On land it eats seeds, tender young plants, and rice.

13–16 inches

Spotted Sandpiper

This is the most widespread sandpiper in North America. In spring and summer you can identify it by its spotted white breast. In fall and winter this bird loses its spots. Watch for the Spotted Sandpiper's habit of bobbing its tail up and down as it walks.

white line above eye

olive-brown head and back

short, straight, pinkish bill has a black tip

dull yellow legs

spotted breast and belly

Winter adult

🏠 **Home** Lives almost anywhere there is water, including beaches, lakes, and ponds. Also lives in fields and on farms, but is most common along riverbanks.

🎵 **Voice** Gives a shrill *peet-weet*. While in flight it repeats *weet*.

🟤 **Food** Eats a lot of insects, also small fish.

7.5 inches

Sanderling

You can see this little bird on the beach, running back and forth as the waves wash up onto the sand and back down. As the water moves off the sand, it exposes sand crabs, which are what the Sanderling mostly eats. When not hunting for food, this sandpiper stands on the beach away from the water. It often will stand on one leg with its head tucked into its back.

rust-colored wash on head, breast, and back

Juvenile

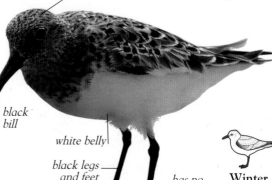

black bill

white belly

black legs and feet

has no hind toe

Winter adult

🌲 **Home** Lives on rocky or sandy seashores and nests on the stony tundra of the Far North.

🎵 **Voice** Gives a harsh *kree*. In flight it cries *twick* or *kip*.

🐦 **Food** Eats sand crabs and other crustaceans, mollusks, marine worms, and insects.

8 inches

Least Sandpiper

Tiny sandpipers such as this one are known as "peeps." This is the smallest sandpiper in North America, and one of the smallest shorebirds in the world. It gathers in flocks that fly together in unison, wheeling, banking, and twisting.

brownish gray head and back

thin, dark bill curves down slightly

white belly

pale green-yellow legs

streaked neck and breast

There are other, more common sandpipers along the coast, but inland this is the one you are most likely to see. It is the only peep with yellow legs.

Winter adult

Home Lives in wetland habitats and along the muddy shores of rivers and ponds.

Voice Gives a high *kneet* or *knee-eet*.

Food Picks small animals from the surface of mud and probes in the mud with its bill for insects, insect larvae, and small crustaceans.

6 inches

Gallinago gallinago

Common Snipe

This sandpiper has a long bill designed to capture prey underground. The bill can bend, which helps the bird feel and catch its prey in the soft mud. The snipe's bill is twice the length of its head. When surprised, a snipe bursts up and flies in a zigzag path. Then it dives straight back to the ground.

eyes set far back on face

distinctly striped head and back

long, thin bill

greenish legs and feet

Home Found near marshes and other wet areas. Nests on the ground.

Voice Makes a scratchy *zhak* call after being surprised and flying into the air. Says *wheat-wheat-wheat* on breeding grounds.

Food Eats worms, insects, and tender roots found in mud and soft dirt.

10–11 inches

Wilson's Phalarope

This bird spins while swimming like a duck in the water – as fast as 60 times per minute. It does this to stir up small creatures from the bottom for food. It also pokes about in mud to find food. Phalaropes are unusual in the bird world because females are more boldly colored than males. They are larger, too.

broad stripe from eye to neck

pale-gray back and wings

white line above eye

Female

brownish-gray back and wings

Male

long, needle-shaped bill

white chin and cheeks

dull-yellow legs and feet

Juvenile

Winter adult

Home Lives near prairie ponds, marshes, lakes, and rivers. Many flock to the Great Salt Lake in migration.

Voice Mostly silent. When breeding it calls *aya*, sounding like a toy whistle. Also honks softly, which sounds like a dog barking in the distance.

Food Eats insects, worms, and other tiny creatures, as well as the seeds of marsh plants.

8–9.5 inches

Larus delawarensi

Ring-billed Gull

One of the most common gulls in North America, this crow-sized bird has adapted well to living near people. It will eat just about anything. It follows plows to find bugs and worms and will steal food from other birds.

yellow bill with black ring

white face and breast

pale-gray back and upper wings

greenish yellow legs and feet

Juvenile

First Winter

Second Winter

Third Winter

It even searches through garbage dumps and begs for food in parking lots. It takes a young bird three years to look like an adult.

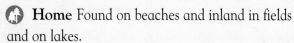

🏠 **Home** Found on beaches and inland in fields and on lakes.

🎵 **Voice** Makes a shrill *ky-ow* or high-pitched *hiyak, hiyak*.

🌙 **Food** Eats worms, insects, and other small animals, as well as grain and garbage.

18–19 inches

California Gull

A monument to this gull can be seen in Salt Lake City, Utah. In 1848 a large flock arrived just in time to eat a swarm of grasshoppers that threatened to destroy the first crops planted by Mormon settlers. It is the state bird of Utah.

white head, neck, and breast

yellow bill with red and black spots near tip

gray back and upper wings

greenish legs

Dark Juvenile

First Winter

Second Winter

It takes two years for the young birds to look like adults.

🏠 **Home** Lives along beaches in the winter. Nests in large colonies near lakes and marshes during the breeding season.

🎵 **Voice** Repeats a soft *kee-yah*. When alarmed, it calls *yowww*.

🦅 **Food** Eats insects and other small animals. Likes to look through garbage for food.

21–22 inches

Herring Gull

This large gull likes to soar high overhead like a hawk. It prefers to nest on the ground, but if people move into its area, it will nest in trees or on roofs. Like other gulls, this bird sometimes will drop clams and other shellfish from the air to break open the shells. Young birds take four years to look like adults.

white head and breast

yellow bill with red spot

Second Winter

Third Winter

black wing tips

light-gray wings and back

pinkish legs and feet

Dark Juvenile

Fourth Winter

🌲 **Home** Common along the coasts, especially in harbors and at garbage dumps. Also lives on rivers and lakes.

🎵 **Voice** Has several noisy calls, including *yucka-yucka-yucka*, *kek-kek-kek*, and a trumpetlike *kee-ow, kee-ou*.

🐟 **Food** Eats fish, worms, insects, and other small animals, as well as berries and garbage.

22–26 inches

Forster's Tern

Like other terns, this bird feeds while flying. It will scoop fish from the surface of the water or dive to catch a meal. Because it prefers to live in marshes, some people call it the Marsh Tern. In winter, the bird's head turns white and the black cap is replaced with a narrow black eye patch.

orange bill with black tip

black cap

pale gray wings and back

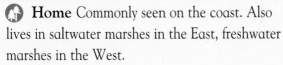

deeply forked tail

orange legs and feet

Juvenile

Winter adult

🌲 **Home** Commonly seen on the coast. Also lives in saltwater marshes in the East, freshwater marshes in the West.

🎵 **Voice** Its call is a low *zrurrr*. It also cries *kit, kit, kit*.

🐛 **Food** Eats insects as well as small fish.

14–15 inches

Pigeon Guillemot

Some people call this bird the Sea Pigeon. In winter, most of the black feathers turn white or gray. The inside of its mouth is bright red. It dives for food and swims underwater, using its wings for paddles. The Pigeon Guillemot likes to nest in the cracks of rocks. Sometimes it digs a hole in a sandy bank for a nest.

solid black body

narrow, pointed black bill

large white wing patch

red feet and legs

Winter adult

🏠 **Home** Likes shallow water near rocky coasts. Also found on the open sea.

🎵 **Voice** Makes a high whistling sound, *peeee*.

🟤 **Food** Dives underwater to eat fish and other small sea creatures found at the bottom.

13–14 inches

Tufted Puffin

The Tufted Puffin, like other puffins, is most at home on the sea. It uses its strong wings to fly and to swim underwater. Like other members of its family, this bird digs a tunnel called a burrow, where it builds its nest. The bird can carry a dozen small fish in its beak back to its chicks. Puffin chicks do not leave the burrow until they are ready to fly.

white face

thick orange bill

yellow tufts behind eyes in breeding season

Juvenile

Winter adult

black body

orange legs and feet

Home Spends most of its time on the ocean. Comes ashore on sea cliffs.

Voice Silent except for occasional growling sounds near nest.

Food Eats fish, squid, and a variety of other small sea animals.

15.5 inches

Phasianus colchicus

Ring-necked Pheasant

The colorful male is easy to spot. The female is mostly brown, so she is better at concealing herself. A pheasant sometimes makes a loud whirring sound when it is flying. It usually flies only a short distance, then lands and runs away. The Ring-necked Pheasant is not native to North America – people brought this bird here from Asia. It is the state bird of South Dakota.

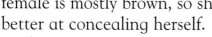

Female

red face wattles

blue-green or purple head

chickenlike yellowish bill

white ring around neck

Male

large bronze body

short legs

long, striped tail feathers

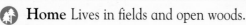

🏠 **Home** Lives in fields and open woods.

🎵 **Voice** Clucks like a chicken. Male also makes a loud *KOCK-cack* call, like a rooster.

🍃 **Food** Eats mostly seeds, grains, and berries. Also eats large insects, such as grasshoppers, as well as mice and snails.

21–36 inches

Greater Sage-Grouse

This plump bird has amazing mating habits. Males gather to "dance." The male struts and dances, spreading his spikelike tail feathers. He has an air sac in his breast that he fills with air, and when he lets the air out it makes a loud bubbling, popping sound. The smaller and plainer female selects a dancing male with which to mate.

long, spiked tail feathers

yellow eyebrows

white ruff

white throat

black belly

Female

Male

black belly

 Home Lives within scrubby vegetation in the open country of the West, usually sagebrush, which is its favorite food.

 Voice Sounds like *kuk, kuk, kuk*.

Food Eats sagebrush and evergreen leaves.

21–30 inches

Willow Ptarmigan

In winter this bird turns white except for its black tail. This helps it hide in the snow. In summer the male is rusty-red, and the female is brown. This helps the birds hide against dark rocks. The feathers on the Willow Ptarmigan's legs and toes act like snowshoes. Male birds stand guard while the females sit on their eggs. This is the state bird of Alaska.

Female

no red eyebrows

gray-brown body

red eyebrows can be hidden

stout black bill

Male

square tail

feathered legs and toes

Winter adult

🏠 **Home** Lives in the arctic tundra. Likes areas with willows and bushes.

🎵 **Voice** During mating season, males bark *go-back, go-back, go-back*.

🍂 **Food** Eats some insects, but mostly tender leaves, buds, and flowers. It especially likes willows.

15–17 inches

Wild Turkey

American colonists enjoyed turkey at the first Thanksgiving feast. Even before then, the turkey was a popular game bird. It seldom flies far and prefers to run from danger. Males are called "gobblers" or "toms." Females are called "jennies." Wild Turkeys roost in trees at night.

fanlike tail

naked blue-and-pink head

red wattle

smaller head

usually has no beard

large, shiny, bronze body

black beard

pink legs

smaller body is duller in color

Female

Male

🏠 **Home** Lives in forests with fields nearby.

🎵 **Voice** Male gobbles. Males and females make *cluk, cluk, cluk* sounds.

🍂 **Food** Eats acorns, seeds, nuts, and berries, as well as insects.

37–46 inches

Callipepla californica

California Quail

Lawn sprinklers and bird food on the ground often attract this bird to neighborhoods and parks. One bird stands guard while other birds eat. Like most land birds, it is most active in the early morning and late afternoon.

black plume

cream forehead

black throat with white border

bluish gray breast

Male

A group of quail is called a covey. These birds explode into flight when surprised. This is the state bird of California.

brown sides with white streaks

shorter black plume

small bill

scaled pattern

Female

Juvenile

🌳 **Home** Lives in brush near open areas, parks, and woodlands.

🎵 **Voice** Calls *ka-ka-kow*, which sounds as if it is saying *chi-ca-go*.

🐦 **Food** Eats mostly seeds, but also fruits, berries, and insects.

10 inches

Rock Dove

Some of the fastest birds in flight, Rock Doves have been used to carry messages. They are different from most birds because they come in different colors. One might be brown, gray, white, or a combination of those colors.

neck feathers shine green, bronze, or purple

short curved bill

blue-gray overall

You will see them in parks and parking lots, on telephone wires, and in many other places near people. The Rock Dove is not native to North America – people brought this bird here from Asia.

Color variations

🏃 **Home** Lives in the city, nesting on buildings or under tall bridges. Likes rocky areas in the wild.

🎵 **Voice** Softly sings, *coo-a-roo, coo-roo-coo*.

🍽 **Food** Eats grass, seeds, and berries in the wild. Likes bread crumbs and other scraps in the city.

13–14 inches

Band-tailed Pigeon

The Band-tailed Pigeon is an aerial acrobat. It flies fast, twisting and turning in the air. This is the largest of the pigeons in North America. It normally lives in forests, but it is moving into cities. Most birds tip their heads up after each sip of water. Pigeons are different. They stick their bill in and suck up water as if they were using a straw.

narrow white band on back of neck

yellow bill with dark tip

purplish gray body

light gray band at end of dark-gray tail

yellow feet and legs

🌲 **Home** Lives mainly in forests but is moving into city parks and gardens.

🎵 **Voice** Sounds like an owl with its call of *oo, whoo-oo, whoo-oo, whoo-oo, whoo-oo, whoo-oo.*

🐦 **Food** Eats acorns, grain, and berries.

14–15 inches

Mourning Dove

This is the most common dove in neighborhoods and farmyards. Its wings make a whistling sound when it flies. It feeds mostly on the ground. Male and female share the job of sitting on eggs. Young doves, called squabs, are fed "pigeon milk," which is made in the crops of both male and female adult birds. The crop is a special food storage organ in the neck of the bird.

Juvenile

black spot on lower cheek

black spots on wings

brownish gray body

pink legs and feet

long dark tail with white edges and tip

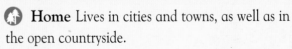

🏠 **Home** Lives in cities and towns, as well as in the open countryside.

🎵 **Voice** Makes a sad-sounding *coo-ooh, coo, coo-coo.*

🍂 **Food** Eats seeds, grains, berries, and insects.

12 inches

Turkey Vulture

When flying, this bird's wings are held up in an angle, not straight across like some other vultures. Groups of vultures soar in circles in the sky. The similar Black Vulture is smaller and has a black head.

small, bald, red head

light bill

large brown-black body

yellow legs and feet

The vulture's strong sense of smell helps it find food. This bird is helpful because it gets rid of dead animals. The Cherokee call the Turkey Vulture the Peace Eagle because it rarely kills anything.

Juvenile

Home Likes open areas but is found in different habitats across North America.

Voice Mostly silent. This bird has no voice box. It may hiss or grunt at others.

Food Eats mostly dead animals.

26–32 inches

Osprey

Also called the "fish hawk," this bird dives into the water feet first to catch fish. It can dive from as high as 100 feet above the water. An Osprey has sharp, curved claws to help it hold slippery fish, which it usually carries head first into the wind as it flies. This is the official bird of Nova Scotia.

mostly white head

white belly

long tail with thin black bands

sharp, curved claws

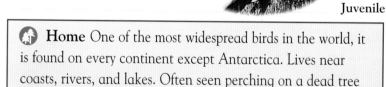

Juvenile

🌲 **Home** One of the most widespread birds in the world, it is found on every continent except Antarctica. Lives near coasts, rivers, and lakes. Often seen perching on a dead tree branch or on large rocks.

🎵 **Voice** Its loud whistles sound like *kyew* or *chewk-chewk-chewk*.

🦅 **Food** Eats fish. On rare occasions it will eat small mammals, birds, or reptiles.

21–24 inches

Bald Eagle

This awesome bird, which lives only in North America, is the US national bird. Although it is known for its white head and tail, young birds, or juveniles, are mostly brown until they are four or five years old. Nesting Bald Eagles add a new layer of loose sticks to the same nest each year. A nest can grow to the size of a king-size bed.

bright-yellow eyes

white head and neck

Juvenile

dark-brown body

wide wings

feathered legs

yellow feet

white tail

🐦 **Home** Lives on the coast and near large lakes and rivers.

🎵 **Voice** Has a squeaky cackle, *kleek-kik-ik-ik-ik* or a lower *kak-kak-kak*.

🦅 **Food** Catches fish with its talons and will eat small mammals and waterfowl. Will steal food from other birds. Also eats dead animals.

34–43 inches

Northern Harrier

Unlike some hawks that hunt high in the sky, the Northern Harrier flies close to the ground and uses its keen sense of hearing to take prey by surprise. In flight this bird shows a white patch of feathers on its back just above the tail, called a rump patch. A harrier often flies with its wings held above its body, which makes the bird look like a shallow V.

gray head and back

Male

gray breast

black wing tips

brown head and back

white belly

very long tail

Female   **Juvenile**

🌲 **Home** Formerly called the Marsh Hawk, this bird lives near marshes and wet meadows, as well as on open grasslands.

🎵 **Voice** Usually silent. You might hear a shrill *kee-kee-kee* when it is near its nest.

🦅 **Food** Eats mainly mice, rats, frogs, and snakes but also eats lizards, crayfish, insects, birds, and dead animals.

16–24 inches

Red-tailed Hawk

This is one of the most common hawks in North America. When it flies, the adult's rust-red, fan-shaped tail makes the bird easy to identify. You are likely to see this bird along a road looking for prey.

rust-red tail

large bill

white belly with broad band of dark streaking

There are five races of this bird that are different colors. One that lives in the Great Plains, called Krider's Red-tailed Hawk, has a pink tail.

Krider's Red-tailed

🌲 **Home** Prefers a mix of open areas and trees. Lives across North America, except on the tundra and deep in forests.

🎵 **Voice** Cry sounds like a squealing pig, *kree-kree ree-e-e-e.*

🦅 **Food** Swoops down to catch mice, rats, squirrels, rabbits, prairie dogs, and other small birds, snakes, lizards, frogs, and insects.

19–25 inches

Golden Eagle

The golden feathers for which this bird was named can be seen best up close, but when the sun shines on it in flight you can see a flash of gold. This huge eagle stands as tall as your kitchen countertop. Wings that open as wide as a man's arms allow it to soar through the air. It swoops down quickly to surprise and catch its prey.

golden feathers on head and neck

brown eyes

dark-brown bill

dark brown overall

feathered legs

yellow feet

Juvenile

🌲 **Home** Lives in mountains, canyons, and other rugged places. Builds its nest on high cliffs or in the tops of tall trees.

🎵 **Voice** Usually silent. Occasionally makes a yelping bark.

🦅 **Food** Hunts groundhogs, marmots, foxes, skunks, minks, rabbits, ground squirrels, birds, tortoises, snakes, and other small animals.

30–40 inches

American Kestrel

This is the smallest and most common falcon in North America. The female, which has a brown back and wings, is not as brightly colored as the male. The kestrel can often be seen perched on utility wires, bobbing its tail as it looks for prey on the ground. If it spots a meal it often stops in midair to hover before swooping down to make the catch.

light breast and belly with streaks

Female

reddish tail with black stripes

two dark lines come down from eyes

reddish back with dark bars

blue-gray wings

spotted tan breast

Male

reddish tail has white tips and one wide black band

🌲 **Home** Lives at the edge of woods, in open fields, along highways, in wooded canyons, and on plains and deserts. Takes over nesting holes other birds have made.

🎵 **Voice** Because this bird says *killy-killy-killy*, some people call it a Killy Hawk.

🦅 **Food** Eats insects, mice, bats, birds, lizards, small snakes, frogs, and other small animals.

9–12 inches

Prairie Falcon

After searching from its perch or
flying low, this hunter swoops down
to capture its prey on the ground.
Sometimes it hovers, like
the American Kestrel,
before striking its
prey from above.
The Prairie
Falcon is a bird
of the badlands,
where it nests on
high cliffs. When
it flies, you can
tell this bird
by its black
"armpits."

dark
markings on
white face

white
eyebrows

brown back
and wing
feathers have
sand-colored
edges

white
throat

light breast
and belly
have heavy
brown spots

legs feathered
halfway to feet

brown tail with
sand-colored
bars

yellow legs
and feet

Juvenile

🌲 **Home** Lives in prairies, deserts, canyons, foothills, and
mountains. Likes open areas where it can fly low to hunt.

🎵 **Voice** Usually silent. When alarmed it
cackles *kek-kek-kek.*

🦅 **Food** Eats small birds such as sparrows and
quail, plus squirrels, prairie dogs, and other small
animals. The young eat large amounts of insects.

15–19
inches

Barn Owl

The heart-shaped "monkey" face and long legs make this owl easy to identify. The well-named Barn Owl is often found in barns, where there are plenty of mice to eat. Like most other owls, this bird hunts at night and sleeps during the day. Although the disks on its face are a different shape from those of other owls, they do the same thing. The disks collect sound waves to help the owl hear better.

dark eyes

no ear tufts

heart-shaped disks on face

long legs

🌲 **Home** Lives in the forest and in open fields. Makes its nest in a tree cavity, building, or cave. Some will use a nest box that people make for them.

🎵 **Voice** Makes a harsh, hissing screech that sounds like *eeeeeeSEEek*.

🦅 **Food** Eats small mammals, such as rodents and shrews. Also eats small birds.

14–20 inches

Western Screech-Owl

ear tufts

gray to brown body with streaking

yellow eyes

heavily streaked breast and belly

You will probably hear this bird more often than you will see it. It is nocturnal—it hunts at night. This screech-owl makes its nest in holes or hollow places in trees. During the winter it stores leftover food in holes. This bird is a little taller than this book, and it does not say *who* like some other owls. Its call is a low, stuttering whistle.

Home Lives in many places, including wooded canyons, deserts, orchards, and neighborhoods.

Voice Gives a series of short whistles on the same pitch, speeding up toward the end.

Food Hunts at night for small animals of all kinds, including mice, frogs, snakes, fish, other birds, and insects.

8–10 inches

Bubo virginianus

Great Horned Owl

This is the most widespread and best-known owl in North America. It is a powerful hunter that will attack animals bigger than itself, even a cat or a dog. Like most owls, the Great Horned is mostly nocturnal, and its wings make no noise when it flies. This is the official bird of Alberta.

yellow eyes

feathers around ears look like horns

rusty patches on face with black edges

barred, brownish gray body

🏠 **Home** Lives in many places, including woods, marshes, mountains, and deserts.

🎵 **Voice** A series of three to eight soft, deep hoots, *Whoo! Whoo-whoo-whoo! Who! Who!* It sounds like "You awake? Me too!" Males and females sometimes sing together.

🦅 **Food** Grabs animals of all kinds with its talons, including mice, rabbits, foxes, skunks, birds, frogs, fish, insects, and even porcupines.

18–25 inches

Snowy Owl

True to its name, which refers to its white coloring, this owl lives in the snowy Far North. Unlike most owls, it

is active day and night and nests on the ground. Its flight is smooth and strong, and it often glides in the air. If there is a shortage of its food, small animals called lemmings, it may go as far south as the United States. This is the official bird of Quebec.

yellow eyes

large round head

dark spots and bars on tips of feathers

Male

Female

more dark bars than on male

all-white body

🏠 **Home** Nests in the arctic tundra. Spends winters along sea coasts, marshes, meadows, lakes, and rivers.

🎵 **Voice** Usually silent. Near its breeding grounds it makes a loud, growling bark, *krow-ow*, or a sharp whistle.

🔴 **Food** Lemmings and mice are its main foods. Also hunts other small mammals, birds, and fish.

20–24 inches

Spotted Owl

You may never see a Spotted Owl, but you have probably heard of this bird. It is nocturnal and keeps to itself, and there are not many of these owls remaining. The Spotted Owl is listed as endangered in the Northwest and threatened in the Southwest. When old forests are cut down for logs, it loses its habitat. The Spotted Owl is a lot like the Barred Owl in shape and size, and sometimes it mates with the Barred Owl.

large, round head

dark brown with white spots all over

Home Lives deep in old forests. Likes canyons and gorges.

Voice Sounds a little like a howling dog, *whoo-whoo-hoo-hoo*. Also has a low, musical whistle, *coooo-wee*.

Food Catches mice and rats with its talons. Also hunts bats, birds, and insects.

16–19 inches

Common Nighthawk

Nighthawks are often seen at dusk, flying around street lights to catch insects. When a male is courting a female, he makes big swooping dives in the air. At the bottom of the dive his wings make a sound like a rubber band being plucked.

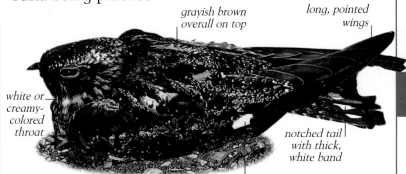

grayish brown overall on top

long, pointed wings

white or creamy-colored throat

notched tail with thick, white band

white wing patch

The nighthawk has coloring that blends with its surroundings, which makes it nearly impossible to see while it is sitting on its nest on the ground.

🏠 **Home** Lives in different habitats across North America – in city and country, woodlands and fields.

🎵 **Voice** Has a froglike call of *peeant* or *beant*. You might hear this bird before you see it.

🌙 **Food** Commonly seen flying around lights at night as it catches huge amounts of insects.

8–10 inches

Common Poorwill

The first part of this bird's scientific name means "feathered moth," because its feathers are as soft as moth wings. The poorwill is the smallest member of the nightjar family.

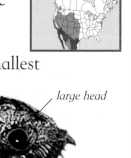

large head

spotted brownish gray or pale-gray body

black throat and sides of face

white tips on black outer tail feathers

broad white band over throat and breast

This is one of the few birds known to hibernate in cold weather like bears do. However, most poorwills migrate south for the winter, where they do not need to hibernate.

Home Lives on mountain slopes and rocky hills, as well as in grasslands and desert.

Voice Cries *poor-will* or *poor-willy* or *poor-willow*, repeated 30 to 40 times per minute.

Food At night flies low to the ground to catch insects such as moths. Also jumps into the air from the ground to catch insects such as grasshoppers.

7–8 inches

White-throated Swift

"Swift" means fast, and this swift is one of the fastest flying birds in North America. The swift is agile, too. It dashes and darts, swoops and twists in the air.

black back

white patch on wings

white chin, throat, and belly

long, narrow wings

long-thin tail

When it is in flight, you can see white patches on its wings and sides. Its black-and-white plumage makes the White-throated Swift easy to identify. Its nest is made of feathers glued together with saliva and placed deep in cracks on rock walls.

Home Lives on coastal cliffs, steep canyons, and mountains, and in valleys.

Voice Two or three birds flying together will loudly cry *he he he he*. Also makes a screechy twitter and trilling call.

Food Has a wide mouth like other swifts, which is how it scoops up and eats insects in flight.

6–7 inches

Calypte anna

Anna's Hummingbird

Like all hummingbirds, Anna's can fly in any direction – forward or backward, up or down. The male is the only "hummer" in North America that has a rose-red crown and throat. Anna's is large for a hummingbird, and it eats more insects and spiders than any other. The male often sings while sitting on a perch.

short, straight black bill

rose-red throat and crown

Male

grayish belly with green tint

green crown

red flecks on throat

green back

pale-gray breast and belly

rounded green tail

Female

Juvenile male

🌲 **Home** Lives in neighborhoods, canyons, and woodlands.

🎵 **Voice** Its sharp, squeaky call sounds like *chick*. When chasing prey, makes a rapid, high-pitched rattle. Sings a mixture of coarse, squeaky notes.

🌙 **Food** Sips nectar of flowers. Catches insects in flight and plucks spiders from webs. Visits feeders for sugar water.

3.5–4 inches

Rufous Hummingbird

Rufous is a rusty-red color, which is how this hummingbird got its name. Fierce for such a small bird, it attacks bigger birds, and even chipmunks, if they enter its territory or try to use its feeder. One of the first to migrate each spring, this bird flies north in February and March. The male's gorget, which is the patch of color on its throat, sparkles copper-red in sunlight.

rufous head and back

straight black bill

orange-red throat

Male

white throat speckled with small spots

metallic green back and wings

Female

🌳 **Home** Lives in woodlands, meadows, and mountains.

🎵 **Voice** Call is a hissing *chewp chewp*. When defending its territory, the male makes a call that sounds like *zeee-chupppity-chup*. Its wings make a buzzy-sounding whistle when the bird is in flight.

🐦 **Food** Sips nectar from flowers and eats many insects. Visits feeders for sugar water.

3.75 inches

Melanerpes uropygialis

Gila Woodpecker

This woodpecker digs a hole into the saguaro cactus for its nest. The Gila Woodpecker is an important part of the desert community, because its empty nest holes provide shelter for other animals such as wrens, snakes, and mice.

small red cap

creamy brown head

creamy brownish breast and belly

black-and-white bars on wings and back

Male

black-and-white bars on tail

no red cap

Female

🌲 **Home** Lives in saguaro deserts, mesas, woods that are near rivers, and cottonwood groves. Often seen around giant cactus. Also lives in cities and towns.

🎵 **Voice** Makes a trilled *churr* and loud, high-pitched *yip* or *pit*.

🦅 **Food** Eats mostly insects, plus cactus fruit and mistletoe berries. Visits feeders for suet or fruit.

8–10 inches

Red-breasted Sapsucker

Sapsuckers drill rows of holes in the trunks of trees. These holes are called "sap wells." The bird then drinks the sap that collects in the wells. This is the only woodpecker species in which the male and female look exactly alike. Red-breasted Sapsuckers sometimes breed with a bird that is similar but has a black bib, called the Red-naped Sapsucker.

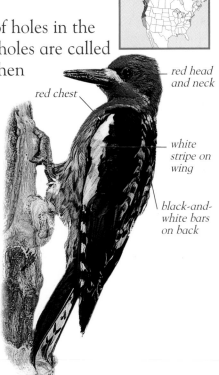

red head and neck

red chest

white stripe on wing

black-and-white bars on back

🏠 **Home** Lives in woodlands and coastal forests.

🎵 **Voice** Often silent. Sounds somewhat like a cat, with a low *meww*. Also cries *yew-ick, yew-ick* and *kew-yew*. Males tap sharply with their bills.

🌙 **Food** Eats tree sap and bark, plus insects that might damage the tree. Also eats fruits and berries. Visits feeders for sugar water and suet.

8–9 inches

Downy Woodpecker

This is the smallest woodpecker in North America. In the spring, the male and the female search together for a place to nest. After making a decision, they tap on the tree of their choice. Every fall, each bird digs a fresh hole in a dead tree, where it will roost. It takes five to eight days to dig a hole. The female looks like the male, except she does not have the red spot on the back of her head.

black crown

short black bill

red patch on back of head

black shoulders

white back

white belly

black wings with white spots

Home Lives almost anywhere there are trees, including suburbs and orchards. Will use a nest box designed for it.

Voice Makes a high-pitched but soft whinny, like a horse. Call is a flat *pik* or *pick*.

Food Digs insects and grubs from bark. Also eats caterpillars, spiders, snails, berries, and nuts. Visits feeders for suet, peanut butter, sunflower seeds, and bread.

6.75–7 inches

Northern Flicker

This bird eats a lot of ants, perhaps more than any other bird in North America. There are two different kinds of Northern Flicker. The "yellow-shafted" bird is yellow beneath its wings and tail. Also called a "yellowhammer," this is the state bird of Alabama. The "red-shafted" is red beneath its wings and tail and has a red mustache. Both have a black crescent bib.

Red-shafted male

red crescent on back of head

brown back and wings with black bars

gray forehead

tan face

black mustache

black spots on pale chest and belly

Yellow-shafted male

🏠 **Home** Lives in woods, neighborhoods, and in the desert. The yellow-shafted bird lives in the East, Canada, and Alaska. The red-shafted bird lives in the West. These birds will nest in birdhouses and nest boxes.

🎵 **Voice** Loudly says *klee-yer* or *clearrrr* and *wicker, wicker, wicker.*

🪶 **Food** Eats mostly ants, often on the ground. Also eats other insects, fruits, and berries.

12.75–14 inches

Geococcyx californianus

Greater Roadrunner

The Roadrunner is a large member of the cuckoo family. It can fly but seldom does – its long legs are built for running swiftly after its prey. When surprised, it runs for cover. Look for a large streaked body, shaggy crest, and long tail. The crest can be raised if the bird is frightened or excited. In spring, the roadrunner often perches on a cactus or tree at sunrise to sing. It is the state bird of New Mexico.

shaggy crest can be raised

heavy, dark bill

reddish, blackish, and white streaks on back and wings

short, rounded wings

long pale-blue legs and feet

long tail with white spots

🌲 **Home** Lives in dry, brushy, open country.

🎵 **Voice** Gives a series of dovelike *coooos* and a low, rolling *preeet-preeet*.

🐦 **Food** Eats a great deal of insects. Also eats rodents, lizards, snakes, and tarantulas. It will eat birds' eggs and fruits such as prickly pears, as well as seeds.

20–24 inches

Belted Kingfisher

Like other kingfishers, this bird has a
bill and head that look too big for its
body. The Belted Kingfisher is
unusual among birds because
the female is more colorful
than the male. She has
a reddish brown band
across her belly,
which the male
does not have. A
kingfisher dives
headfirst into
the water for
its prey.

Female

reddish
brown band
on belly

reddish brown
sides

white spot in
front of eye

shaggy
crest

white
collar

blue-gray
wings
and back

long, thick
black bill

blue-gray band
across breast

white belly

Male

🦅 **Home** May be found wherever there is water – lakes,
rivers, ponds, bays, mountain streams, and creeks.

🎵 **Voice** Makes bold, raspy rattle sounds, like a
heavy fishing reel.

🌑 **Food** Eats mostly small fish. Also eats frogs,
tadpoles, crayfish, small snakes, and insects.

11–14.5
inches

Pacific-slope Flycatcher

This bird is found along the Pacific Coast in moist canyons. The very similar Cordilleran Flycatcher lives in the mountains farther inland. Both species migrate to Mexico and Central America for the winter. When identifying both species, the tear-shaped eye ring and completely yellow belly are important field marks.

large olive-green head

tear-shaped pale eye ring

light-colored wing bars

yellowish belly

dark-gray legs and feet

brownish green back

brownish gray wings

long brownish gray tail

🏠 **Home** Lives in moist shady forests and canyons along streams. Migrates to Mexico and Central America.

🎵 **Voice** Male sings a slurred, high-pitched, thin *psee-yeet*, whistled on a rising scale and usually repeated three times.

🌕 **Food** Eats insects such as ants, bees, wasps, and caterpillars. Also eats some berries and seeds.

5.5 inches

Black Phoebe

Phoebes, which are members of the flycatcher family, have a habit of slowly pumping their tails up and down. A phoebe often hunts from a low, shaded branch or fence post. It watches for insects, then swoops to catch them in the air. The Black Phoebe is generally found near water. It sometimes will snatch insects or small fish from the water's surface.

black bill

black body

black breast

white belly

black legs and feet

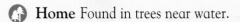

Home Found in trees near water.

Voice Most common call is a sharp *seek!* Sings four notes, *pee-wee, pee-wee.* The first *pee-wee* goes up, the last goes down. Also makes a loud *tsee.*

Food Eats mostly insects, including bees, ants, beetles, moths, and caterpillars. Eats fruits and berries in winter, when insects are hard to find.

6–7 inches

Pyrocephalus rubinus

Vermilion Flycatcher

Vermilion, a shade of red-orange, describes the male bird – the most colorful flycatcher in North America. This bird may live in dry areas, but it is most often found near whatever water may be there, such as ponds, irrigation ditches, or cattle tanks. It has a habit of wagging its tail up and down.

red crown

dark-brown back and wings

black bill

dark blackish brown tail

dark mask

red chest and belly

Male

Juvenile male

white chin and throat

some light red or pink coloring on belly

Female

🏠 **Home** Lives in trees near water sources or roadsides.

🎵 **Voice** Call is a piercing, thin, metallic *pseeup*. When courting, the male sings a soft tinkling *pit-a-see! pit-a-see!* then a rapid *pi pi-li-li-li-sing* while hovering with his crest raised and tail spread.

🐦 **Food** Catches flying insects. Also picks insects such as beetles and grasshoppers off the ground.

6 inches

Western Kingbird

Kingbirds are members of the flycatcher family. The Western Kingbird is the most common and well-known kingbird in the West. It usually builds its nest in a tree but also will use utility poles and fence posts. It often hunts while perched on utility wires or fences. You might see it hover before it dips down to snatch up food. This bird will chase hawks, crows, and other larger birds from its nesting area.

pale-gray head

black bill

olive-green back

grayish white throat and breast

bright lemon-yellow belly

black legs and feet

white edges on black tail

🌲 **Home** Lives in open country around towns, ranches, and prairies. Also can be found in trees along streams.

🎵 **Voice** Call is a short *bek*. Also chatters *ker-er-ip, ker-er-ip, pree pree pr-prr.*

🐦 **Food** Catches flying insects such as bees and moths, plus insects on the ground such as crickets and caterpillars. Eats some fruits and berries.

8.75 inches

Scissor-tailed Flycatcher

Beautiful and graceful, Oklahoma's state bird is named for the way it opens and closes its long tail like a pair of scissors. The male does an amazing "dance" in the sky during courtship. First he flies high into the air, then dives. Then he flies in a zigzag pattern while making a trilling cackle. Next he flies straight up again and falls over backward, doing two or three somersaults.

pale-gray head

white throat, chest, and belly

salmon-pink sides show in flight

long, forked black-and-white tail

Young birds look similar to adults but have shorter tails.

🌲 **Home** Perches on trees and utility wires or fences along country roads, ranches, or prairies.

🎵 **Voice** A harsh, sharp *bik* or *kew*. Calls also include a dry, buzzing, chattering *ka-quee-ka-quee* or repeated *ka-lup*.

🐦 **Food** Catches insects in the air or from the ground. Also eats small fruits and berries.

11.5–15 inches

Loggerhead Shrike

Nicknamed the "Butcher Bird," this hunter perches on wires and fences to watch for a meal. From there, it swoops down and catches prey. Insects are the shrike's favorite food, but it might catch a small rodent, bird, or snake. The shrike has an unusual habit of sticking its prey on a sharp thorn or a barbed wire spike. Sometimes the bird tears its food apart there, and sometimes it saves the food for later.

large bluish gray head

hooked black beak

bluish gray back

black mask

black wings with white patch

black tail with white outer feathers

Juvenile

🏠 **Home** Lives in open areas along roadsides, orchards, grasslands, open woods, and hedges.

🎵 **Voice** Usually silent but makes a variety of squeaky notes and low warbles. Often repeats *queedle, queedle.* Its call is a grating *shak-shak.*

🍴 **Food** Eats small animals, including mice, small birds, insects, frogs, and snakes.

9 inches

Tachycineta thalassina

Violet-green Swallow

Like most swallows, this bird lives and feeds in flocks. It often catches insects high in the air, and the Violet-green Swallow can also be seen swooping low over water.

shiny greenish black back and wings

greenish black wings

notched tail

white coloring on cheek extends above eye

white breast and belly

A swallow's bill opens very wide so it can act as an insect trap while the bird flies through the air.

Juvenile

🏠 **Home** Lives in forests, woods, and sometimes neighborhoods. Nests in dead trees or old woodpecker holes.

🎵 **Voice** Makes slightly buzzing *chi-chit* noises. The male repeats *tsip, tsip* when he is flying during courtship, just before sunrise.

🌑 **Food** Catches insects while in flight, such as flies, bees, wasps, beetles, moths, and leafhoppers.

5 inches

Barn Swallow

Farmers welcome this bird because it
eats insects that might destroy their
crops. Like other swallows, the Barn
Swallow feeds while in flight. A flock
often nests
together
in a cave,
under a
bridge, or in
a barn. That is
how they got
their name. This
swallow is easy to
tell apart from
other swallows by
its deeply forked
tail and deep-
blue back.

*shiny blue-black
neck, back, and
top of wings*

*reddish
brown
forehead*

*reddish
brown
throat*

*chest and
belly can
be white
or orange*

*long, deeply
forked tail*

Juvenile

🏠 **Home** Lives in open country. Often found nesting on
farms, under bridges, and on cliffs along lakes.

🎵 **Voice** Repeats a short *chi-dit, chi-dit* or *wit-
wit*. Its song is a long, twittering warble.

🐛 **Food** Catches insects in the air, such as
dragonflies and moths. Follows farmers' plows to
catch grasshoppers, crickets, and other insects.

**6–8
inches**

Steller's Jay

The only jay in the West with a crest, this bird was named for the Arctic explorer Georg Wilhelm Steller, who discovered it in 1741. Jays are in the same family as crows, ravens, and magpies. This family contains some of the boldest, noisiest, and most active birds in North America. Steller's Jay even imitates the calls of hawks. It was chosen as the official bird of British Columbia.

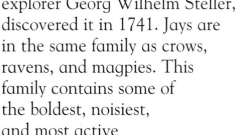

black head, crest, and neck

black back

long, straight bill

smoky blue belly

blue rump

blue wings and tail with black bars

black legs and feet

🌲 **Home** Lives mostly in forests and woods.

🎵 **Voice** Has many calls, including a harsh *shaack, shaack, shaack* and *shooka, shooka*, or a mellow *klook klook klook*. Often imitates the calls of other birds.

🐦 **Food** Eats a variety of animals, such as frogs, snakes, birds' eggs, and insects. But mostly eats pine seeds, acorns, and fruits. In winter, often visits feeders for nuts, seeds, suet, or peanut butter.

11–12 inches

Western Scrub-Jay

Like other members of the crow family, the Western Scrub-Jay is bold, noisy, and active. It likes to perch on posts, trees, or wires to see what is going on. It sometimes will take food, especially peanuts, from a person's hand. Scrub-Jays help plant oak forests, because they bury acorns to save and eat later.

white eyebrow over dark eye patch

dark blue head

gray back

white throat outlined with blue

blue wings

blue band on chest

whitish belly

long blue tail

Home Lives in scrub lands, woods, parks, and yards.

Voice A noisy bird, its call is a hoarse, repeated *shreep* or *quay-quay-quay*.

Food Eats acorns, nuts, grains, fruits, insects, spiders, birds' eggs, mice, lizards, frogs, and other small animals. Will come to bird feeders for nuts, cracked corn, sunflower seeds, suet, or bread.

11 inches

American Crow

Simply called a crow by most people, this bird is one of the most widespread and well-known birds in North America. Family groups travel and feed together. Their diet includes a wide variety of food items. Crows are smart birds and are not fooled by scarecrows. Fearless and lively birds, they are often seen diving at hawks in the air. They like shiny things and may pick up a shiny object to take back to the nest.

brown eyes

black bill

solid black body

black legs and feet

short, fan-shaped tail

🏃 **Home** Lives wherever trees grow – in woods, on farms, and in neighborhoods.

🎵 **Voice** Most people know its loud *caw-caw*. It also has a begging call that sounds like *uh-uah*.

🦜 **Food** Eats animal and plant foods, including insects, spiders, snails, frogs, snakes, young birds and birds' eggs, worms, clams, dead animals, grains, fruits, and seeds.

17–18 inches

Common Raven

This member of the crow family is the largest perching bird in North America. The raven seems to truly enjoy flying and at times appears to be playing in the air. This bird is smart and sometimes works as a team with other ravens to hunt for food. You might see ravens looking for scraps of food at picnic areas. This is the official bird of the Yukon Territory.

solid black body

long, thick bill

shaggy throat feathers

long, wedge-shaped tail

black legs and feet

🏡 **Home** Lives in a wide variety of places, including mountains, forests, beaches, deserts, and canyons.

🎵 **Voice** Has several calls. Some are musical, but most are a croaking *croooaaak* or *cur-ruk,* or a metallic *tok.*

🍖 **Food** This scavenger eats dead animals, frogs, worms, insects, young birds and birds' eggs, mice and other small animals, and also berries.

24–26 inches

Pica hudsonia

Black-billed Magpie

This unusual bird, with its very long
tail, is easy to spot. It can be confused
with only one other bird, the Yellow-
billed Magpie, which lives in California.
You can tell the two apart by the color
of the bill. Magpies are members of
the crow family. The Black-billed
Magpie sometimes sits on
cows or elk to eat ticks off
them. This bird builds
a large nest of mud
and sticks, with
a roof and
two holes.

heavy
black bill

black
back

white patches
on upper
wings

black breast

white belly
and sides

black-and-
white flight
feathers

very long tail with
green highlights

🌲 **Home** Likes scattered trees in open country, trees beside
streams, or open fields.

🎵 **Voice** A noisy bird, it chatters *chuck-chuck-chuck*. It
also says *mag*, and may give a musical whistle.

🍴 **Food** Hops or walks on the ground, hunting
for insects such as grasshoppers. Also eats dead
animals, birds' eggs and chicks, mice, snakes, some
fruits, and grains.

17–22
inches

Horned Lark

This songbird spends most of its time on the ground. However, the male performs a wonderful flight to impress a female. He flies high, then – while singing – he closes his wings and drops, headfirst, almost to the ground. At the last second he opens his wings to keep from crashing.

hornlike black tufts

white or yellowish face and throat

black mask

brown back and wings

black bib

white belly

black tail with white outer feathers

Then he perks up the hornlike feathers on his head, droops his wings, and struts around the female. Horned Larks form big flocks in winter.

🌲 **Home** Nests on the ground in open areas, such as fields, plains, tundra, airports, or beaches.

🎵 **Voice** Sings a series of bell-like, tinkling notes, *pit-wee, pit-wee*. Calls *tsee-tete* or *zeet*.

🐦 **Food** Runs or walks over the ground, eating seeds, grain, and insects such as grasshoppers.

7–8 inches

Poecile rufescens

Chestnut-backed Chickadee

The Chestnut-backed Chickadee is named for the chestnut-brown color of its back. This active little bird often feeds high in the trees, and it sometimes hangs upside down while eating. You might also find this bird on the ground looking for insects.

chestnut-brown back

white cheeks

grayish brown cap

lighter chestnut-brown on sides

If the female is disturbed on her nest, she makes hissing sounds.

short black bill

black bib

white breast and belly

dark-gray legs and feet

🌲 **Home** Lives in evergreen forests along the West Coast.

🎵 **Voice** Its song is not whistled like that of other chickadees. Instead it sounds like *chip-chip-chip*. Has a rough, rapid call that sounds like *tseek-a-dee-dee*.

🐦 **Food** Eats insects, caterpillars, and spiders and their eggs. Also eats seeds from evergreen trees. At feeders it will eat cracked corn, sunflower seeds, and suet.

4.75 inches

Oak Titmouse

In most of the areas where it lives, the Oak Titmouse is the only plain, gray-brown bird with a crest. The bird can raise its crest or hold it down. There is a similar bird called the Juniper Titmouse, which is more gray (less brownish) and lives farther east than the Oak Titmouse.

short crest

small black bill

gray-brown back

lighter gray face, breast, and belly

gray-brown wings

dark-gray feet and legs

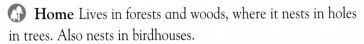

🌲 **Home** Lives in forests and woods, where it nests in holes in trees. Also nests in birdhouses.

🎵 **Voice** Call is *tschick-a-dee*. Sings a repeated series of high and low notes that sound like *pee-chee, pee-chee, pee-chee*.

🐦 **Food** Eats a variety of seeds, especially acorns, plus insects that it picks from trees. Attracted to sunflower seeds and suet at feeders.

5.25 inches

Red-breasted Nuthatch

To protect its young from other animals, a nuthatch smears sticky sap around the entrance to its nest. The nuthatch digs a hole in a tree for its nest, or uses an old woodpecker hole. These birds often walk down a tree trunk head first. To break open the shell of a seed, a nuthatch wedges it into a crack in the bark, then hammers with its bill.

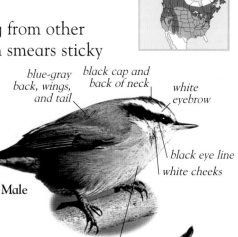

blue-gray back, wings, and tail

black cap and back of neck

white eyebrow

black eye line

white cheeks

Male

reddish brown breast and belly

lighter cream-colored breast

Female

🏠 **Home** Lives in woods and forests. Will use birdhouses.

🎵 **Voice** Its high-pitched call of *ank, ink,* or *enk* sounds like a tiny tin horn, often repeated in a rapid series.

🐦 **Food** Eats seeds, especially seeds from pine trees. Will eat some insects, such as moths, beetles, wasps, and caterpillars. Will come to feeders for suet, chopped nuts, and sunflower seeds.

4.5 inches

White-breasted Nuthatch

This is the largest nuthatch in North America. Nuthatches often creep down a tree trunk head first. They circle around and beneath branches, looking for insects under the bark.

black cap and nape

long black bill

blue-gray back

white face and breast

white patches in blue-black tail

orange-brown lower belly

white belly

black feet and legs

After the White-breasted Nuthatch visits a bird feeder, it may hide seeds in a crack or crevice to save them for later meals.

Home Lives in woods and forests. Nests in holes in trees. Will nest in birdhouses.

Voice Sings *wee-wee-wee-wee-wee-wee-wee*, getting higher with each note. Its call is a hoarse *yank-yank-yank*.

Food Eats acorns, hickory nuts, beechnuts, and corn. Also eats moths, caterpillars, ants, flies, grasshoppers, and wood borers. Visits feeders for sunflower seeds, mixed seeds, and suet.

5–6 inches

Certhia americana

Brown Creeper

The Brown Creeper roosts hanging onto the trunk of a tree or the side of a house with its sharp claws. Like a woodpecker, it has stiff feathers in its tail which it uses to brace itself. Watch how the Brown Creeper goes up a tree searching for insects to eat. Looking almost like a mouse, it circles around the trunk as if going up a spiral staircase to the branches.

long, thin, curved bill

white line over eye

white breast and belly

sharp claws

brown back with buff streaks

long reddish brown tail with stiff feathers

Home Lives in woods, forests, and wooded suburbs.

Voice Makes a musical *see-see-tit-see*. Its call is a soft, thin *seee*.

Food Eats insects such as aphids, beetles, caterpillars, and spiders. Some visit feeders for peanut butter, suet, and chopped peanuts.

5.25 inches

Cactus Wren

The state bird of Arizona is the largest wren in North America. The Cactus Wren often builds a domed

nest in the spiky cholla cactus. The cactus needles, or the sharp spines of yucca, protect the eggs and young birds. This bird eats mostly insects. It hunts for them on the ground by lifting objects with its bill. Unlike most wrens, this bird rarely holds up its tail, and it looks more like a thrasher than a wren.

broad white stripe over eye

brown cap

reddish-brown, streaked back and wings

long, curved bill

heavy black spots on breast

white band on tail

whitish belly with spots

🐾 **Home** Lives in dry areas among yucca or mesquite.

🎵 **Voice** A low *guah guah guah guah guah*, which gains speed toward the end.

🐦 **Food** Eats mostly insects but also fruits, berries, lizards, and frogs. Will visit feeders for bread, sliced apple, or potatoes.

8.5 inches

House Wren

This plain bird may be small, but it is bold. The House Wren will invade the nests of other birds and break their eggs or kill baby birds. The male builds several nests each spring in almost any crack or container.

narrow, pale eye ring

grayish brown back

thin black bars on tail and wings

thin, slightly curved bill

pale-gray breast and belly

thin, dark bars on sides and lower belly

The female House Wren then chooses which nest she wants to use and lays her eggs there. Like most wrens, the House Wren hops about with its tail held up.

Home Lives in woods and brushy areas, on farms, in parks, and in neighborhoods. Will nest in birdhouses.

Voice Sings a beautiful, trilling, flutelike song. Repeats this gurgling melody after a short pause. Its call is a rough, sharp *cheh-cheh* or a sharp chatter.

Food Eats mostly insects, such as ants, grasshoppers, bees, and caterpillars. Also eats spiders, millipedes, and snails.

4.75 inches

American Dipper

The dipper is named for the way it stands beside a stream and quickly raises and lowers its body as if it is doing deep knee bends. Like ducks, dippers have oil on their feathers to keep them strong in the water. They use their wings to "fly" underwater, and they can fly straight into the air from underwater. A dipper may even walk on the bottom of a stream looking for food. This is the only dipper in North America. It is the only songbird that swims regularly.

white eyelid

stubby tail

straight black bill

slate-gray overall

pinkish legs and feet

Juvenile

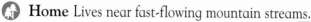

🌲 **Home** Lives near fast-flowing mountain streams.

🎵 **Voice** Song is a long series of warbles, buzzes, and trills. Call is a loud, shrill *zzreip, zzreip* or *rreip*.

🐦 **Food** Eats insect larvae found in water, such as those of mayflies and mosquitoes. Also eats water bugs and worms, clams, and young fish.

7.5 inches

Regulus calendula

Ruby-crowned Kinglet

The small red patch on the male Ruby-crowned Kinglet's head is usually hidden. When he gets excited, he raises the feathers on his head, and the red flashes. A similar bird called the Golden-crowned Kinglet has a yellow patch with a black border on its head.

no red patch on top of head

white eye ring

two white bars on wings

Female

small red patch on top of head, often hidden

olive-green back

short black bill

white eye ring

white or creamy olive breast and belly

Male

🏠 **Home** Lives in forests. Also seen in wooded yards.

🎵 **Voice** Sings a series of high-pitched *tsee, tsee* notes, followed by several *tew* notes, then a three-note call of *liberty-liberty-liberty*. It is very loud for such a small bird. Also says *je-ditt* and *cack-cack*.

🐦 **Food** Searches for insects in trees. Also eats berries and seeds.

4.25 inches

Blue-gray Gnatcatcher

Look for the Blue-gray Gnatcatcher near the tips of branches in tall trees.

This bird is small and slender, with a long, thin bill and blue-gray feathers. Like other gnatcatchers, it has a habit of pumping its tail up and down or wagging it from side to side. It will sometimes fly out from a perch to catch flying insects.

long black tail with white outer feathers

blue-gray head and back

black line over eye in breeding plumage

white eye ring

Male

white breast and belly

no black line above eye

lighter blue-gray back and head

Female

🏠 **Home** In the East, lives in moist woods. In the West, likes thick bushes or open, dry woods.

🎵 **Voice** Sings a low-pitched, trilling *zee-you, zee-you*. Its call, *pwee?* or *speee?*, which sounds like a question, is heard more often.

🐛 **Food** Eats insects and their eggs and larvae.

4 inches

Sialia mexicana

Western Bluebird

The Western Bluebird likes to nest in a hole facing an open area, so farms and golf courses are good places for bluebird houses. The number of bluebirds had been decreasing because there are fewer large old trees in which they can nest. People are building bluebird boxes for their nests, and bluebirds are making a comeback.

blue throat and head

rust-colored breast and sides

bright-blue back and wings

Male

brownish gray back

pale-gray throat

grayish white belly

bright-blue tail

blue-gray tail and wings

Female

🏠 **Home** Likes pastures and open woods.

🎵 **Voice** Male's song is *f-few, f-few, faweee*. Also calls *pa-wee* or *mew*.

🐛 **Food** Catches insects in the air or on the ground. Also eats spiders, snails, and berries. Visits feeders for peanut butter, suet or cornmeal mixtures, mealworms, currants, and raisins.

7–7.75 inches

Mountain Bluebird

This bird's all-blue coloring sets it apart from other bluebirds. It lives on tree-covered mountains in summer, but in winter it moves down the mountain where it is warmer. It hovers more than other bluebirds and sometimes catches insects while flying. It also pounces on insects on the ground. This is the state bird of Idaho and Nevada.

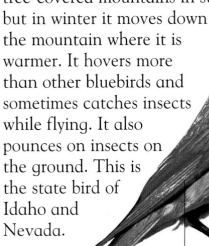

pale-blue breast

Male

white belly

turquoise blue overall

dull brownish gray overall

Female

🌲 **Home** Likes open areas with scattered trees on mountains, in pastures, meadows, and aspen groves. Nests in holes in trees.

🎵 **Voice** Often silent. Song is a low, warbling *tru-lee*. Call sounds like *phew*.

🐦 **Food** Eats mostly insects, including weevils, beetles, cicadas, ants, grasshoppers, and crickets. Also eats grapes and berries.

7 inches

Catharus guttatus

Hermit Thrush

This is the only brown-backed spotted thrush you might see during winter. Important field marks to look for are the reddish brown tail and the bird's habit of slowly raising and lowering its tail. You are most likely to see a Hermit Thrush by itself on the ground, searching for food. This is the state bird of Vermont.

white eye ring

dark eye

olive-brown head and upper back

cream-colored throat and breast with brown spots

reddish brown tail and lower back

grayish belly with light spots

pinkish feet and legs

Home Lives mostly at the edge of woods and forests.

Voice Known for its beautiful song of long, clear, low flutelike notes, then delicate ringing tones, ending in thin, silvery notes. Calls *chuck*, often *chuck, chuck*. Also cries *whee*.

Food Eats insects, berries, small fruits, worms, and snails.

6.75 inches

American Robin

The return of the robin is thought to be a sign that spring has come. But the robin stays year-round in many areas. You may see a robin turn its head to the side while it hops on the ground. People once thought the bird was listening for worms. The real reason that the robin tips its head is so it can better see the worms. This is the state bird of Connecticut, Michigan, and Wisconsin.

blackish head

yellow bill

broken eye ring

dark brownish gray back

brick-red breast

Male

white lower belly

Juvenile

brownish gray head

brownish orange breast

Female

🏠 **Home** Lives all over in woods, fields, meadows, parks, towns, and neighborhoods. Uses nesting shelves and birdbaths.

🎵 **Voice** Sings a gurgling, slow, sing-song *cheerily cheer-up cheerio*, often repeated. Rapidly calls *tut-tut-tut* or *hip-hip-hip*.

🍴 **Food** Eats worms, insects, fruits, and berries. Visits flat feeders for chopped nuts, suet, or fruits.

10 inches

Northern Mockingbird

The mockingbird sings its best on warm, moonlit nights. It imitates the songs of other birds, as well as other sounds. It has even been heard barking like a dog. A mockingbird protects its territory and will swoop at people, cats, and dogs – even its own reflection in a window. The mockingbird has a habit of flicking its tail. This is the state bird of Arkansas, Florida, Mississippi, Tennessee, and Texas.

thin, dark line through eye

gray head and back

long, dark tail with white outer feathers

large white patches on dark wings

two white wing bars

Juvenile

Home Lives in scrubby woodlands, desert brush, canyons, farms, parks, and neighborhoods.

Voice Sings a variety of its own songs and imitates other birds. Repeats phrases three to five times. Has a loud, harsh *check* call.

Food Eats insects, spiders, crayfish, lizards, berries, and fruits. Visits feeders for peanut butter, chopped nuts, suet, bread, and raisins.

10 inches

Sage Thrasher

Thrashers are named for their habit of thrashing about, tossing up leaves with their bills while they look for insects. The Sage Thrasher likes to nest in large sage bushes. This bird's bill is not as long or as curved as those of other thrashers. The Sage Thrasher has the shape and some of the habits of a mockingbird, including the habit of flicking its tail.

yellow eye

brownish gray head and back

cream-colored breast and belly with black streaks

two white wing bars, which often fade by spring

white corners on tail

Home Lives in dry areas such as sagebrush plains and rocky canyons. Looks for scrub and thickets in cold weather. Nests in large sagebrush.

Voice Sings pleasant, warbled phrases that change all the time, although the bird often repeats them. If alarmed it says *chuck-chuck*.

Food Eats many insects, plus fruit and berries.

8–9 inches

Curve-billed Thrasher

This is a common desert bird. Like other thrashers, it is often seen digging in the ground with its bill, looking for food. The Curve-billed Thrasher often sings from the top of a cactus or calls loudly from a perch in mesquite. This thrasher builds its nest in the fork of a cholla cactus or in yucca, mesquite, or mistletoe.

grayish brown
head and back

orange
eyes

long
curved
bill

cream-colored
breast and
belly with
faint spots

darker gray tail

🌲 **Home** Lives in desert scrub, thickets of thorny shrubs, and neighborhoods. Nests in large cactus and mesquite.

🎵 **Voice** Musical song varies, often with low trills and warbles. Has a sharp call, *whit-wheet*.

🐦 **Food** Eats fruits, berries, seeds, and insects. This bird is attracted by water, such as a birdbath or dripping faucet.

11 inches

European Starling

About 60 European Starlings were brought over from Europe and released in New York in 1890. This was part of a project to bring to America every bird mentioned in William Shakespeare's plays. Since then, starlings have spread to all of the United States and much of Canada. These birds gather in large flocks that are noisy and messy. They damage crops and compete for nesting sites with other birds that nest in holes.

black body with purple-green gloss (speckled white in fall and winter)

short tail

yellow bill with blue base (female has pink bill)

pinkish legs

Juvenile

Home Lives in cities, neighborhoods, orchards, woods, and on farms and ranches. Nests in birdhouses.

Voice Sings trilling melodies, clear whistles, clatters, and twitters. Imitates other birds and machine sounds. Also makes a flutelike *pheeEW*.

Food Hunts on the ground for insects. Also eats worms, fruits, berries, seeds, and grain.

8.5 inches

Bombycilla cedrorum

Cedar Waxwing

The Cedar Waxwing tends to travel in flocks. You often find 50 or more of them feeding in trees or bushes with berries. Sometimes you see the waxwing on the ground, picking up fallen berries or drinking from a puddle. This bird is called a waxwing because there are hard, waxlike red tips on some of its wing feathers. Waxwings have been seen passing a berry or flower down a row of birds, from one to the next, until one of the birds eats it.

pointed crest

black mask and chin

grayish brown back

pale-yellow belly

waxlike red tips, often not seen

pointed wings

white under tail

yellow band at end of tail

Juvenile

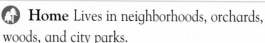

Home Lives in neighborhoods, orchards, woods, and city parks.

Voice Call is a thin, high *zeeee* or *zeeeet*.

Food Eats fruits, berries, flower petals, maple tree sap, and insects. It is attracted to yards with mountain ash and cedar trees.

7 inches

Orange-crowned Warbler

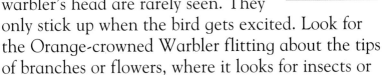

The orange feathers on top of this warbler's head are rarely seen. They only stick up when the bird gets excited. Look for the Orange-crowned Warbler flitting about the tips of branches or flowers, where it looks for insects or probes for nectar with its bill. It usually nests on the ground. The faint streaks on its side and yellow coloring under the tail are the best ways to tell it apart from a young Tennessee Warbler.

olive-green head and back

faint line through eye

paler yellowish green breast and belly

Home Lives in thickets at the forest's edge.

Voice The male sings a high trill, *chip-ee, chip-ee, chip-ee,* which gets higher or lower, and often slower, near the end. Has a rough-sounding call of *stic.*

Food Eats insects, spiders, and nectar. Visits hummingbird feeders in winter. In the East, it also visits feeders for suet and peanut butter.

5 inches

Dendroica coronata

Yellow-rumped Warbler

This warbler remains farther north in winter than other warblers. Even when the male's feathers change color in the winter, this bird can be identified by the patch of yellow on the rump. You might see this bird in big flocks. Eastern birds have white throats, and western birds have yellow throats.

streaked back

Female

streaked breast and belly

two white wing bars

yellow patch on crown

Male

yellow rump

streaks on sides

black face patch

black on breast

yellow side patches

Fall adult

Winter adult

 Home Lives in woods, forests, and wooded yards.

Voice Various slow warbles that slow down in the middle, then speed up. Each song ends with either rising or falling notes. Some have a musical *trill*. Call is a loud *check, chup,* or *chip.*

Food Eats mostly insects, but will eat berries and seeds. Visits feeders for sunflower seeds, suet, or peanut butter.

5.5 inches

Common Yellowthroat

Look for the Yellowthroat close to the ground in wild, tangled areas, such as briers, cattails, or overgrown creek banks. The female looks plain and can be difficult to tell from some other female and juvenile warblers. The Yellowthroat has a habit of flicking its tail and drooping, then flicking, its wings. This is one of the most widespread warblers in North America.

black mask with whitish border on top

greenish gray head, back, and wings

Male

bright-yellow throat and breast

white belly

Juvenile

pale eye ring

pale-yellow breast and throat

Female

Home Lives in marshes, meadows, and other moist areas with thickets.

Voice Its song sounds like *wichity wichity wich*, and it can vary. Sharp, raspy calls of *chuck* or *djip*. Sometimes gives a flat *pit*.

Food Eats insects and spiders.

5 inches

Wilsonia pusilla

Wilson's Warbler

This warbler is generally found close to the ground. It picks insects off low branches in wet woodlands and bogs. You may also see it flit into the air to catch insects.

grayish green back and wings

black cap

long grayish green tail

Male

bright-yellow face, breast, and belly

grayish green head

dull yellowish gray face

The Wilson's Warbler has a habit of jerking its tail up and down or around in circles while it eats.

Female

🌲 **Home** Lives in moist thickets along streams and bogs, and in woods.

🎵 **Voice** Song is a quick series of slurred *chee-chee-chee* notes, dropping lower at the end. Rough, nasal *chimp* call.

🐦 **Food** Picks small insects and spiders off leaves and catches them in the air.

4–5 inches

Western Tanager

When it is summer in the western mountains, this is one of the most colorful birds you might see. The male has a bright-red head that turns yellow in the fall and winter, when his coloring looks more like that of the female. The female has an olive-gray back, and she is dull in color. A juvenile bird looks like the female but has dark-brown streaks on its feathers.

red head and throat

black back

black wings with two bars

Male

yellow belly

olive-gray back

Winter male

Female

🌲 **Home** Lives in the forests of the western mountains.

🎵 **Voice** Sings a lot, sounding like *che-ree, che-ree, che-weeu, cheweeu*. Calls *pit-ick, pri-tick-tick*.

🐦 **Food** Eats fruits and insects, even wasps and bees. Catches its food in the air or picks insects off trees and the ground. Visits feeders for pieces of fresh oranges, dried fruit, and bread crumbs.

7 inches

Pipilo maculatus

Spotted Towhee

Some people confuse towhees with American Robins. However, the Spotted Towhee has reddish brown only on the sides. The American Robin has a solid reddish brown breast.

blackish head and chest

white spots on back

two white wing bars

long tail

reddish brown sides

Male

white belly

Towhees are often seen near bushes, scratching for insects in fallen leaves, pulling both legs back at the same time. Towhees are related to sparrows.

dark-brown head and breast

dark-brown back

dark-brown wings with two white bars and white spots

Juvenile

white tips on outer tail feathers

Female

🌲 **Home** Lives in woods, thickets, gardens, and parks.

🎵 **Voice** Makes two *chip* notes, followed by a trill. Along the coast this bird only does the trilling part, fast or slow. Has a slurred, mewing *guee* call.

🌑 **Food** Scratches for insects in fallen leaves under shrubs. Also eats seeds and fruits.

7–7.5 inches

Canyon Towhee

Towhees are shy birds, found low in brush or on the ground. They scratch about on the ground to uncover food. The Canyon Towhee and the California Towhee look so much alike that people once thought they were the same species. You can tell them apart by song and location. The map on this page shows where you will find the Canyon Towhee. The California Towhee lives in parts of California and southwest Oregon.

reddish brown cap

streaks on throat

cream-colored eye ring

dark center spot on breast

whitish patch on belly

grayish brown body

rusty red under long tail

🌲 **Home** Likes lower slopes of mountain canyons covered with brush, juniper, or pinion.

🎵 **Voice** Makes one or two *chips*, followed by *chwee, chwee, chilly, chilly, chilly*, getting faster as it goes. Its call is a slurred *chedep* or *chee-yep*.

🌘 **Food** Eats grain, seeds, and insects. Visits yards for seeds and cracked corn on the ground.

8 inches

Spizella passerina

Chipping Sparrow

Named for its song – a series of chipping sounds – this bird likes to sing from a high perch. Sometimes it sings at night as well as during the day. The Chipping Sparrow is often found near people. Nests have been found in yards and cemeteries and on golf courses.

heavy white line over eye

bright reddish brown cap

thin black line through eye

gray cheek and neck

clear gray breast and belly

long, notched tail

two white wing bars

streaked brown-and-black back and wings

This bird often joins a flock with other sparrows in the winter.

Juvenile

Winter adult

🌲 **Home** Lives at the edges of woods and in brushy pastures, parks, orchards, and neighborhoods. Likes pine trees.

🎵 **Voice** Repeats a series of trilled chip notes, *chip-chip-chip-chip-chip-chip-chip*, all in the same pitch. Has a call of *seek*.

🐦 **Food** Eats mainly seeds, especially grass seeds. Also eats insects. Will peck at salt blocks. Visits feeders for bread crumbs and seeds.

5.5 inches

Lark Sparrow

This sparrow sings while flying, while perched, and even at night. The male sings and struts with his tail spread out to attract a female. The female builds her nest on the ground. If disturbed, she runs away with her wings fluttering and tail spread. This leads the predator after her and away from her eggs. The Lark Sparrow is often found in flocks.

black, white, and reddish brown stripes on head

reddish brown patch on face

white mustache

streaked back and wings

whitish breast

tail has white tips and outer feathers

Juvenile

🌲 **Home** Likes fields, savannah, farms, woods, and parks.

🎵 **Voice** Its long, happy, bubbling song starts with two loud, clear notes followed by a series of chips, buzzes, and trills. Repeats its sharp, metallic *tik* call.

🐦 **Food** Often feeds in small flocks on the ground, eating seeds, grasses, and insects. Will visit yards for small grains placed on the ground.

6–7 inches

Calamospiza melanocorys

Lark Bunting

In spring the Lark Bunting forms large flocks on the prairie. The flock appears to roll by as birds from the back of the flock fly to the ground ahead of the other birds, looking for food. When claiming his territory, a male Lark Bunting flies straight into the sky while he sings.

Male

Winter adult

black or slate-gray overall

bluish gray bill

large white wing patches

streaked gray-brown overall

bluish gray bill

Then he flutters back down to the ground. This is Colorado's state bird.

white wing patch

Female

Home Found on prairies, plains, and meadows.

Voice Song is a flutelike, warbling melody of full whistles and trills. Often sings in groups. Call is *hoo-ee*.

Food Finds insects on the ground, including grasshoppers, ants, beetles, and weevils. Also eats the seeds of dandelions, gooseweed, and grass, as well as grain left in farmers' fields.

7 inches

Savannah Sparrow

yellow or white eyebrow stripe

heavy streaks on breast and sides

pinkish feet and legs

short, notched tail

You might think this bird was named for the grassy habitat where it lives. However, it was named for the city of Savannah, Georgia, where Alexander Wilson discovered it in 1811. There are at least 17 races of Savannah Sparrows. So, this bird can look slightly different in various areas. Look for this sparrow on the ground, where it spends most of its time looking for food.

🏠 **Home** Likes open areas such as savannah, hay fields, salt marshes, wet meadows, and tundra.

🎵 **Voice** Song begins with two or three *chip* notes, followed by two buzzy, insectlike trills, *tip-tip-seeeee-saaaay*. Its call is *seep*.

🐦 **Food** Scratches on the ground for food, including seeds, grasses, insects, spiders, and sometimes snails.

5–6 inches

Song Sparrow

The Song Sparrow sometimes sings for as long as two hours at a time. That is how this bird got its name. This sparrow varies in size and color from very light to very dark races. One thing they all have in common is that they pump their tails when they fly.

streaked brownish gray body

broad grayish eyebrow

white throat

streaked breast

long, rounded tail

pinkish feet and legs

The Song Sparrow is usually found alone or in pairs. In winter, it may flock with other birds.

Dark race

Home Might be found anywhere, but seems to especially like brushy areas near water.

Voice There are differences among birds, but the song is one of the best ways to identify this sparrow. It whistles two or three clear notes, followed by a *trill*. Has calls of *chimp* or *what*, and a high, thin *ssst*.

Food Eats seeds, insects, berries, and fruits. Visits feeders for birdseed.

6–7.5 inches

White-crowned Sparrow

This bird is most often seen under bushes, scratching with both feet at the same time as it looks for food. In winter, it may be seen in flocks with other types of birds. The feathers on the top of this bird's head can be tan on young birds rather than black and white. This coloring is seen in places where the White-crowned Sparrow lives year-round.

white crown with black stripes

pink or yellow bill

back streaked with brown and black

whitish throat

two white wing bars

gray breast

Juvenile

First winter

🏠 **Home** Lives in brushy fields, at the forest's edge, and along streams.

🎵 **Voice** A sad, whistled *poor-wet-wetter-cee-zee*. Calls *pink* or a sharp *tseek*.

🦅 **Food** Eats mostly weed seeds and grasses. Also eats young plants in gardens. Visits yards for cracked corn and seeds placed on the ground.

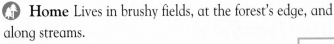

6.5–7.5 inches

Dark-eyed Junco

Small flocks of juncos are usually seen eating and hopping on the ground, looking for food. Sometimes you find them in low bushes. Notice their white outer tail feathers when they fly. Juncos build their nests on the ground in hidden places, such as under fallen logs. There are five races of the Dark-eyed Junco. Juncos are in the sparrow family.

brownish gray head and back

Slate-colored female

Pink-sided male

dark-gray head and back

White-winged male

Gray-headed male

Slate-colored male

white outer tail feathers

Oregon male

🏠 **Home** Lives in woods, brushy areas, fields, and yards.

🎵 **Voice** Musical trill, varied in pitch and speed, from *chip* notes to bell-like sounds. Call is a rough *dit* with a smacking sound. Twitters while in flight.

🐦 **Food** Eats seeds, nuts, grains, and some insects. Visits flat feeders for seeds and nuts.

6 inches

Pyrrhuloxia

This bird's name is pronounced Purr-uh-LOX-ee-ah. When a Pyrrhuloxia flies, you can see red on the undersides of its wings. It spends much of its time hopping around on the ground, looking for seeds and insects.

large red-tipped crest

short, thick bill

gray head and back

Male

red face, throat, and upper breast

red on gray wings and tail

The bill of this bird changes from yellow in summer to gray in winter. It is related to the similar Northern Cardinal, which is red all over with a black mask.

yellowish breast with no red

browner wings and tail

Female

🐦 **Home** Lives in thorny thickets and mesquite brush.

🎵 **Voice** Rich, loud whistles that sound like *chewee, chewee, chewee* or *wheat-wheat-wheat*. Has a sharp, metallic *plik* or *chink* call.

🪶 **Food** Eats seeds and insects. Helps cotton farmers by eating cotton worms and boll weevils. Visits yards for sunflower seeds and birdbaths.

8–9 inches

Pheucticus melanocephalu

Black-headed Grosbeak

Like other grosbeaks, this bird uses its powerful bill to crack open seeds. The Black-headed Grosbeak defends its nesting area from other grosbeaks in summer. When migrating to Mexico and Central America in winter, it often forms flocks. They search for food in trees, in bushes, and on the ground. Males and females sometimes whisper soft songs while they sit on their eggs.

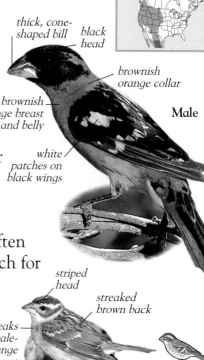

thick, cone-shaped bill

black head

brownish orange collar

brownish orange breast and belly

white patches on black wings

Male

striped head

streaked brown back

streaks on pale-orange breast

Female

Juvenile male

🌲 **Home** Lives in woods, orchards, and gardens.

🎵 **Voice** Rich, back-and-forth series of warbled phrases. Female sings less than male. Call is a high, squeaky *plik*.

🌑 **Food** Eats seeds, berries, and insects. Visits feeders for sunflower and other seeds.

7–8.5 inches

Lazuli Bunting

A male Lazuli Bunting looks a lot like a male bluebird, but bluebirds do not have wing bars. The male Lazuli Bunting may perch high to sing and announce his territory. He flutters his wings to attract a female. But this bird is also seen on the ground or in bushes. After nesting season the Lazuli Bunting joins flocks of sparrows and other buntings.

grayish brown head and back

two pale wing bars

grayish blue rump

blackish wings

Female

turquoise head, throat, and back

brownish orange upper breast

Juvenile

blackish tail and wings

two wide white wing bars

white belly

First spring male

Male

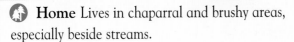

🌲 Home Lives in chaparral and brushy areas, especially beside streams.

🎵 Voice Sings various phrases. Some of these are in pairs and sound buzzy, like *see-see-sweet, sweet-zee-see-seer*. Call is a sloppy-sounding *plik*.

🐦 Food Eats insects, seeds, grains, and grasses.

5–6 inches

Leucosticte tephrocoti

Gray-crowned Rosy-Finch

This bird likes to nest high on the highest mountains, where it hides its nest among rocks on the ground. A Rosy-Finch has a pouch in its throat that it uses to carry lots of seeds back to its babies. This bird walks, instead of hops, as it searches for food on the ground.

black forehead

gray crown

dark-brown back

pinkish wings and rump

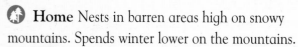

pinkish belly

It is usually seen looking for food near patches of snow.

Juvenile

🏠 **Home** Nests in barren areas high on snowy mountains. Spends winter lower on the mountains.

🎵 **Voice** Long series of high chirps. Calls are a high *chew*, a rough *pert*, and a high-pitched *peent*.

🦜 **Food** Eats mostly seeds but also some insects.

6 inches

House Finch

The House Finch once lived only in the West. In the 1940s, some of these birds were taken to New York as pet birds in cages. Some escaped or were set free. Now they live all over North America. The House Finch often nests in potted plants. In the East it nests in spruce trees found in yards. It might also nest in holes in trees or in a birdhouse.

reddish crown

streaked brown back and wings

Male

bright-red bib

two thin white wing bars

streaked brown sides

streaked brown head, back, and wings

two whitish wing bars

brown streaks on cream-colored breast and belly

Female

🌲 **Home** Lives in many places, including cities, desert brush, orchards, and yards.

🎵 **Voice** Near the nest it makes a *witchew, witchew, witchew.*

🌰 **Food** Eats weed seeds, fruits, blossoms, buds, and insects. Visits feeders for thistle, sunflower, millet, and other seeds.

6 inches

Loxia curvirostra

Red Crossbill

It is easy to see how this finch got its name. The tips of its bill cross instead of coming straight together. This bill works well to pry seeds from pine cones. Young birds have straight bills when they hatch. Their bills grow crooked soon after they leave the nest. The Red Crossbill is unusual because it may nest at any time of year, depending on the pine cone crop.

large head

Male

dark wings and tail

bill crossed at tips

brick-red body

short notched tail

large head

gray throat

dark wings

dusky, creamy-yellow body

Female

Juvenile

🌲 **Home** Lives in pine forests and visits pine trees in yards.

🎵 **Voice** Series of two-note phrases followed by a trilled warble that sounds like *jitt-jitt-jitt-jitt, jiiaa-jiiaa-jiiaaaaa*. Songs can vary.

🐦 **Food** Eats mostly pine seeds but also insects. Visits feeders for sunflower seeds.

5.5–6.5 inches

Pine Siskin

The Pine Siskin looks a little like a sparrow with yellow wing bars. Siskins search for seeds on pine, hemlock, spruce, alder, and birch trees. The Pine Siskin is a very active bird that gathers in large flocks in the winter and is often found in flocks with goldfinches and other birds. Siskins can wander far from their normal range in winter.

streaked brown head, back, and wings

thin bill

white breast and belly with brown streaks

yellow edges on wing flight feathers

yellow at base of tail

notched, dark tail

🌲 **Home** Lives in evergreen forests and woods.

🎵 **Voice** Husky, twittering warble, rising and falling in pitch with an occasional *ZZZzzzzzrree!* that sounds like a tiny chainsaw. Call is rising *tee-e*. Flight note is hoarse *chee* that lowers as the bird goes.

🐦 **Food** Eats seeds, flower buds, and insects. Visits feeders for mixed seed, sunflower seed, and thistle seeds. Enjoys birdbaths.

4.5–5 inches

Carduelis psaltria

Lesser Goldfinch

Flocks of goldfinches search for seeds in fields and low trees. They especially like thistle seeds. Goldfinches often line their cup-shaped nests with thistle down. The Lesser Goldfinch is more attracted to water than most birds. It may stop at a dripping faucet for a drink. In some areas the male Lesser Goldfinch has a black back.

dark greenish back

black cap

bright-yellow breast and belly

white wing patch

white wing bar

no black cap

Male

Black-backed male

notched tail

dull-yellow breast and belly

Female

Juvenile male

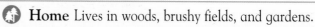

🌲 **Home** Lives in woods, brushy fields, and gardens.

🎵 **Voice** Warbling, twittering series of *swee* notes. Calls are a mewing *tee-yee* and drawn-out, nasal *zweeir*.

🦜 **Food** Eats weed seeds, other seeds, and insects. Visits feeders for thistle, sunflower, and mixed seeds. Enjoys birdbaths.

4.5 inches

American Goldfinch

In the breeding season, the male is bright-yellow and black. In the winter, he turns dusty brown with black wings and tail and looks more like the female. Goldfinches' favorite food is thistle seeds. Sometimes they visit flower gardens to eat the seeds of zinnias and other flowers. Goldfinches travel in flocks. This is the state bird of Iowa, New Jersey, and Washington.

Male

black cap

bright-yellow body

black wings with two white wing bars

black-and-white tail

greenish gray back

dull-yellow breast and belly

Female

Juvenile

Winter male **Winter female**

Home Likes trees with seeds, weedy fields, and thickets.

Voice A jumbled series of musical warbles and trills, often with a long *baybee* note. Its flight song sounds like *per-chick-oree* or *po-tato-chips*.

Food Eats seeds, berries, and insects. Visits feeders for thistle seeds and sunflower seeds.

5 inches

Coccothraustes vespertinus

Evening Grosbeak

During courtship the male feeds the female. Then he dances in front of her. The Evening Grosbeak stays in flocks all year, migrating south and east in the winter in search of food. Noisy groups of grosbeaks are often seen at bird feeders. Grosbeaks are members of the finch family.

gray head and back

white wing patch

Female

black-and-white tail

yellowish gray belly

yellow forehead

thick bill

yellow-and-brown body

black-and-white wings

Male

black tail

Juvenile

🏠 **Home** Found in forests, woods, and neighborhoods.

🎵 **Voice** Series of clipped, warbled phrases, ending with a shrill, whistled note. Calls are loud, piercing *clee-ip, peeer,* and *chirp.*

🦜 **Food** Eats seeds, especially of spruce, fir, and maple. Also eats some buds, berries, and insects (especially spruce budworms). Visits feeders for sunflower seeds. Attracted to salt.

8 inches

House Sparrow

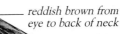

This bird originally lived in Europe. Some were set free in New York in the 1850s. People hoped they would eat canker worms that were hurting trees in city parks. Because the House Sparrow adapts easily to new habitats, especially near people, it quickly spread across North America. The House Sparrow builds nests in gutters and cracks in buildings and can be found in places other birds avoid.

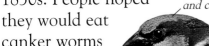

gray crown and cheeks

reddish brown from eye to back of neck

streaked brown wings

black bill

black bib

white wing bar

Male

gray sides and belly

cream-colored eyebrow

Winter male

dark stripe behind eye

no black bib

brownish gray breast and belly

Female

Home Lives in cities, towns, and yards, as well as on farms and ranches. Likes to nest in birdhouses.

Voice Makes a twittering series of *chirps*. Its call is a plain, repeated *cheep-cheep-cheep*.

Food Eats insects, fruits, seeds, and grains. Visits feeders for bread, seeds, and grains.

5.5–6.5 inches

Dolichonyx oryzivorus

Bobolink

The male sings its name, *bob-o-link*, in a happy song. Many birds have lighter colored feathers on their belly and darker colored feathers on their backs. The Bobolink is different. Some people say the male Bobolink looks as if he is wearing his suit backward. These birds gather in large flocks of hundreds of Bobolinks, which sweep across fields. They are nicknamed Ricebirds because they often eat rice crops.

front of head is black

black bill

black breast, belly, and wings

back of head is creamy yellow

large white shoulder patch

white rump

Male

pointed black tail feathers

striped head

streaked back, wings, and sides

pinkish bill

Winter male

Female

🏠 **Home** Found in farmlands, meadows, and prairies.

🎵 **Voice** Lively, bubbling series of notes, starting low then bouncing up, *bob-o-link, bob-o-link, pink, pink, pank, pink*. Call is clear *pink*.

🐦 **Food** Eats weed seeds, grass seeds, rice, grains, and insects.

6–8 inches

Red-winged Blackbird

This common, widespread bird is often found in fields and marshes. In late summer and winter, the Red-winged Blackbird joins cowbirds, grackles, and starlings to form flocks of thousands of birds. They swarm down, like a noisy black cloud, and fill trees or lawns. A flock can cover a whole neighborhood block. The birds hop or run across the ground, trying to get their share of food.

red shoulder patch with yellow edge

sharp, pointed bill

Male

black body

First year male

tan stripe over eye

whitish breast and belly with streaks

streaked brown back and wings

Female

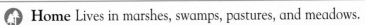

🌲 **Home** Lives in marshes, swamps, pastures, and meadows.

🎵 **Voice** Gurgling, reedy *konk-la-ree* or *gurr-ga-lee*. Calls are a low *clack*, a sharp nasal *deekk*, and a metallic *tiink*.

🦅 **Food** Eats mostly weed seeds and grains, plus insects, berries, snails, and mollusks. Visits yards for bread and birdseed.

7.5–9.5 inches

Western Meadowlark

The Western Meadowlark is a loud, brightly colored bird that sings many songs. It is the state bird of Kansas, Montana, Nebraska, North Dakota, Oregon, and Wyoming. In the winter meadowlarks join small flocks. They build their nests and feed on the ground. The similar Eastern Meadowlark is found farther east.

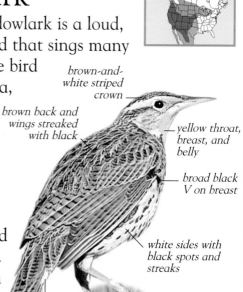

brown-and-white striped crown

brown back and wings streaked with black

yellow throat, breast, and belly

broad black V on breast

white sides with black spots and streaks

white outer tail feathers

Home Found on plains and prairies, in parks, and along grassy streets in towns.

Voice Repeats bubbling, flutelike notes, varying in length, *shee-oo-e-lee shee-ee le-ee*, getting faster at the end. Calls *chuk*. In flight it cries *whew*.

Food Eats mostly insects and spiders. Also eats seeds, grains, and tender green plants.

9–11 inches

Yellow-headed Blackbird

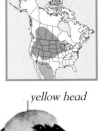

No other bird can be confused with a male Yellow-headed Blackbird. His yellow head makes him easy to find. The female blends in more easily with other blackbirds in flocks. The Yellow-headed Blackbird always weaves its nest in plants that hang over the water. Groups of these birds nest in the same area. However, a male often fights to defend his small territory.

yellow head

black body

yellow throat and breast

white wing patch

Male

brown crown

brown body

brownish yellow breast

brown belly with white streaks

Female

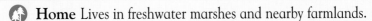

🐦 **Home** Lives in freshwater marshes and nearby farmlands.

🎵 **Voice** High-pitched, raspy, honking gurgle, ending with a lower buzz, *klee-klee-klee-ko-kow-w-w-w, w, w, w.* Call is a hoarse *ka-aack.*

🐦 **Food** Walks in mud or in fields hunting insects, snails, spiders, seeds, and grains.

9–11 inches

Brewer's Blackbird

This bird joins huge flocks with other blackbirds in the winter. Blackbirds sometimes follow plows or tractors on farms to eat the insects these machines turn up. Usually, this bird builds its nest on the ground, but nests have been found high in trees. When it is walking, a Brewer's Blackbird bobs its head forward in short, jerky movements.

purplish shine on head and neck

yellow eyes

greenish blue shine on body and wings

black body

Male

green shine on wings and tail

dark-brown eyes

dark gray-brown body

Female

Fall male

🏠 **Home** Lives in open areas such as pastures, parks, golf courses, and lawns. Also found in savannah, mountain wilderness, marshes, and along Pacific Coast beaches.

🎵 **Voice** Gives a breathy, creaky *ke-see*. Its call is a gruff *check*.

🐦 **Food** Eats mostly insects, such as crickets, grasshoppers, termites, aphids, and caterpillars. Also eats weed seeds, grains, and fruits.

9–10 inches

Common Grackle

Grackles eat, roost, and nest in a group all year. In winter, the Common Grackle can be found in huge, noisy flocks with thousands of blackbirds, starlings, and cowbirds. When a male Common Grackle wants to impress a female, he fluffs out the feathers on his shoulders, droops his wings, and sings.

pale-yellow eyes

purple or bronze shine on back

long, sharp bill

purplish shine on head, neck, and breast

long tail

glossy black body

purple shine on head and neck

Male

dull black body

Female

🏠 **Home** Found in fields, parks, farms, woods, and lawns. Also lives near marshes.

🎵 **Voice** Squeaky *coguba-leek* sounds like a creaking rusty hinge. Call is a bold *chuk*.

🐛 **Food** Eats many foods, including insects, worms, minnows, crayfish, frogs, salamanders, mice, small birds and birds' eggs, seeds, grains, acorns, nuts, and fruits. Visits yards for cracked corn, seeds, and grains placed on the ground.

11–13.5 inches

Great-tailed Grackle

This long-tailed bird sometimes turns into the wind so its tail feathers do not get ruffled. The Great-tailed Grackle searches for food on the ground or in shallow water. Males sing, bob, and bow to impress females.

purple shine on head and back

flat top of head

black body

golden-yellow eye

purple shine on breast

very long tail

Male

yellowish white eye

The female chooses which male will be her mate. They nest in small groups. Grackles are in the same family as blackbirds.

dark-brown head, back, wings, and tail

lighter brown breast and belly

Female

Home Lives in open areas with a few trees, marshes, farms, thickets, parks, and towns.

Voice Makes loud chatters, squeaks, gurgles, shrieks, and whistles. Has a high-pitched squeal that sounds like *may-reee, may-reee*. In flight it calls *chak*.

Food Eats fish, frogs, snails, insects, shrimp, small birds, small reptiles, fruits, grains, and seeds.

10.5–18.5 inches

Brown-headed Cowbird

A cowbird never raises its own young. The female lays a single egg in the nest of another bird, often tossing out the other bird's eggs. Even if some of the original eggs remain, the young cowbird often hatches first. By the time the others hatch the cowbird is older and bigger, so it usually gets more food from its foster parent than the others do. Once the cowbird leaves its foster nest, it will join a flock with other cowbirds and blackbirds.

brown head

short, thick bill

black body with faint green sheen

Male

brownish gray head and back

lighter brownish gray breast and belly

Female

Juvenile

🌲 **Home** Found in fields and pastures. Also lives in parks, woods, and yards, and along streams.

🎵 **Voice** Courtship song is a gurgling *glug-glug-glee*. A female calls with a harsh rattle. A male in flight has a high, slurred *ts-eeeu*.

🐦 **Food** Eats grains, seeds, insects, and berries.

7–8 inches

Hooded Oriole

Orioles weave hanging baskets for their nests. The Hooded Oriole is often seen feeding or nesting in palm trees. It uses its long bill to get nectar and insects from inside flowers. This bird's head might be either bright orange or bright yellow, but all males have a black bib. Females do not.

pale yellow-green head

greenish gray back

Female

two white wing bars

dark olive-green tail

white-edged gray wing feathers

yellow-green belly

orange head

black back

long, curved bill

black on face and bib

two white wing bars

orange belly

Male

white-edged black wing feathers

long black tail

Winter male

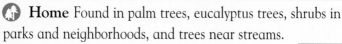

Home Found in palm trees, eucalyptus trees, shrubs in parks and neighborhoods, and trees near streams.

Voice Throaty, warbled whistles with scattered chatter notes. Call is a whistled *wheat* that gets higher. Also makes a series of chatters.

Food Eats insects and nectar. Visits feeders for fruits and sugar water.

7–8 inches

Bullock's Oriole

Orioles spend most of their time in trees and bushes, searching for food among the leaves. They build a bag-like nest that hangs from a branch.

Male

black back

black cap and neck

orange face with black stripe through eye

black bib

orange breast and belly

black tail with orange edges

black wings with large white patch and white edges

If other birds come too close, the parent birds attack. Bullock's Oriole is related to the similar Baltimore Oriole, which lives in the East.

dark-brown wings with two white bars

olive-brown back

yellow face and breast

gray belly

olive tail

First spring male

Female

🐾 **Home** Found in woods, parks, yards, and savannah.

🎵 **Voice** Clear single and double whistles with some gruff or scratchy notes. Has rough, nasal call of *cheah*, given alone or in a series. Also makes a loud rattle.

🍂 **Food** Eats mostly caterpillars and insects but also fruits, berries, and nectar. Visits feeders for oranges, suet, and sugar water.

7–8 inches

Glossary

Adapt - to change to fit into a new place.

Aphid - a small insect that sucks the juices from plants.

Binoculars - a telescope you hold up to both eyes to make objects appear closer and larger.

Bird of prey - a bird that hunts other animals for food; an eagle or owl, for example.

Breed - *verb,* to produce baby birds.

Breeding grounds - where a bird nests and raises its young.

Breeding plumage - a bird's feathers during spring and summer, at which time the bird is mating and raising young birds. In many species, the breeding plumage has brighter colors than the plumage of fall and winter.

Burrow - *noun,* a tunnel or hole in the ground.

Camouflage - feathers, clothing, or fur with a color or pattern that blends into a background.

Canyon - a narrow valley with steep sides.

Chaparral - a thick area of bushes or shrubs.

Colony - a group of birds that live close together.

Conservation - the protection and improvement of natural resources to protect plants and animals for the benefit of everyone.

Contour feathers - the feathers found on the bird's body.

Courtship - when a male tries to attract a female.

Covey - a small flock of birds; quail, for example.

Crest - a pointed tuft of feathers on a bird's head.

Crop - 1. A special sack in the throat of birds, used mainly to store food. 2. Plants grown on farms.

Crown - the top of the head.

Crustaceans - a class of small animals that have an outer shell and usually live in the water; includes shrimp and crabs.

Dabble - the feeding method of some ducks; from the surface of the water, the duck tips up its rump and sticks its head into the water to reach plants and seeds.

Dabbling duck - a duck that feeds from the surface of the water by tipping up its rump and putting its head in the water.

Down - small, fluffy feathers that grow underneath the contour feathers of a bird.

Endangered - a species that is in serious trouble and could face extinction in the near future. It is against the law to own or hurt an endangered species.

Family - a group of bird species with many things in common.

Fledgling - a young bird that is learning to fly.

Flight feathers - long feathers on the wings and tail that help a bird fly.

Flock - *noun*, a group of birds traveling or feeding together. *Verb*, to gather in a group with other birds.

Forage - to look for food.

Habit - a tendency to act in a certain way; a repeated activity.

Habitat - the natural home of a bird or other animal, or the characteristics of an area, including its climate and plants.

Hibernate - to spend the winter in a deep sleep.

Hover - a special type of flight that allows a bird to remain in one place in the air while feeding or while looking for a meal.

Imitate - to copy another bird's song or behavior.

Larvae - the first stage of an insect's life, when it looks like a worm.

Lemming - a small mammal that lives in the Arctic and looks a little like a mouse. Lemmings are a favorite food of the Snowy Owl.

Marmots - a group of thick-bodied mammals with short, bushy tails, about the size of a cat. Marmots, including woodchucks and groundhogs, live in burrows.

Mesa - an area of high, flat land with steep slopes.

Migrate - to move from one area to another as the seasons change.

Migration - the process of moving from one place to another as the seasons change.

Mimic - to copy the song or calls of another bird.

Molt - to shed old feathers and replace them with new feathers. Most birds do this a few at a time.

Morph - one color phase of a bird.

Nape - the back of the neck.

Nest box - a birdhouse or other man-made structure provided for birds to nest in.

Nocturnal - active and feeding at night.

Perch - *verb*, to rest on a branch or other object. *Noun*, a branch, wire, pole, or other object on which a bird sits.

Pesticide - a poisonous chemical used to kill weeds or insects.

Phrase - two or more notes that make up a short section of a song.

Pigeon milk - a substance produced in the crops of both male and female doves and pigeons that is fed to their young birds.

Pitch - how high or low a sound is.

Plumage - feathers.

Prey - an animal killed for food by another animal.

Race - a distinct group within a bird species, marked by some difference. The feather color, eye color, bill color, or song may be different.

Range - the full area in which a bird can be found.

Roost - *verb,* the name for a bird's rest or sleep period.

Ruff - a band of feathers around a bird's neck that it can fluff up.

Rump - the area just above the tail on the back of a bird.

Savannah - an open plain with no trees.

Scrub - short, scraggly trees or bushes growing close together.

Secretive - shy; tends to hide.

Shelter - a place that provides protection from the weather and predators.

Silhouette - the outline of a bird, seen against bright light, so all you see is its shape.

Species - a specific kind of plant or animal. A group of birds that are alike and can produce babies are members of the same species.

Suet - beef fat. Often suet is melted into grease and mixed with cornmeal or birdseed to make suet cakes, which make good food for birds.

Talons - long, sharp claws.

Territory - an area a bird claims as its own.

Threatened - a species that is in trouble and may become extinct if steps are not taken to help it. It is against the law to own or hurt a threatened species.

Throat pouch - a bag like flap of skin under the chin of some bird species. It may be used to attract a female, carry food, or cool off.

Trill - a rapid series of notes, a warbling sound.

Tundra - large areas in the Arctic regions that are mostly flat and have no trees.

Warm-blooded - having a body temperature that stays the same, no matter what the surrounding temperature is.

Wattle - bumpy skin, without feathers and often brightly colored, on the heads of some birds, including turkeys and pheasants.

Index

Picture Credits
Abbreviations: m = male, f = female, b =
bottom, t = top, c = center, l = left, r = right.
Plumage illustrations: Simone End, Carl Salter.
Profile illustrations: Svetlana Belotserkovskaya
151f. **Jacket photographs:** Front: Ron Austing
Tufted Puffin; **Rick & Nora Bowers** Western
Screech-Owl; **Brian E. Small** Western Tanager;
Tom Vezo Steller's Jay; **Telegraph Colour
Library:** J P Fruchet, grass; Back: Mike
Danzenbaker Anna's Hummingbird. **Inside
photographs: Fred J. Alsop III** 141. **Ron Austing**
16, 17, 18, 21, 23, 26, 27, 29m & f, 31m, 33m,
34m & f, 35m & f, 36m & f, 37, 39, 40, 42, 44, 45,
50, 52, 54, 55, 56m & f, 59m & f, 61, 65, 67m & f,
68, 70m & f, 71, 72, 74, 75m, 76, 77, 80f, 81m &
f, 84, 85, 87m & f, 93, 95, 98, 101, 104m & f, 105,
107, 108, 110m & f, 111m, 115m & f, 116, 118,
119, 120, 121, 122m & f, 123m & f, 128, 129,
133, 134m & f, 139m & f, 143m & f, 144m & f,
145f, 146f, 147m & f, 150m, 153m & f, 154f. **Rick
& Nora Bowers** 73, 127. **Mike Danzenbaker** 48,
62, 78, 80m, 83, 94, 109, 150f. **DK Picture
Library/**Dennis Avon 63; Mike Dunning 66;
Frank Greenaway 69; Cyril Laubscher 19, 60m,
64, 145m; Karl & Steve Maslowski 106, 113f,
132, 146m; Kim Taylor 30m & f; Jerry Young 75f.
Kevin T. Karlson 28, 31f, 32m & f, 41, 43, 97,
130f. Brian E. Small 20, 25, 33f, 38, 46, 47, 49m
& f, 53, 57m, 60f, 88, 92, 99, 100, 102, 103, 111f,
112m & f, 113m, 117, 124m, 125m & f, 126f,
130m, 135m & f, 136m & f, 137m & f, 138, 140m,
142m & f, 151m, 154m, 155m & f. Tom Vezo 22,
24, 51, 57f, 58m & f, 86, 89, 90m & f, 91, 96, 114,
124f, 126m, 148, 149m & f, 152m & f. **Vireo/**H.
Clarke 79. Richard Wagner 82m & f.